This book was curated by
Jabbar "Cash" Coleson
Director of Culture & Public Relations
and
Donny Carrington
Creative Director & Media Consultant

Dear Financial Athlete,

Thank you for your interest in Championship Finances: The Rules of Financial Efficiency. May this book be a source of inspiration as you navigate your financial journey. My aim in writing this book is to prepare financial athletes for the "GAME" of life and to help others avoid the pitfalls I faced in adulthood regarding personal finance.

There were unique challenges writing this book, the first being personal finance is "personal" and HIGHLY subjective—making the information seem scattered, inconsistent, and hard to agree on. With so many varying philosophies amongst financial experts, professionals, and gurus, it's no surprise that a book like this hasn't been written yet. But I got you! After all, what would life be without challenges? So, I planted this book as a flag in the sand to give readers a new perspective and a general road map surrounding personal finance, financial efficiency, and percentage-based budgeting.

After many years of life experience, blood, sweat, and tears, Championship Finances hopes to build a community for the next generation of financial athletes. It truly took the hard work, discipline, and dedication of an athlete to bring this book to life. Please consider, as you may not agree with all the content in this book, use the concepts as a general guide to challenge the way you think about personal finance.

T.R.O.F.E. NATION
Let's GOOO!!

"I'm not back, I'm better!"
— Sha'Carri Richardson

TROFE NATION

CHAMPION$HIP FINANCE$

THE RULES OF FINANCIAL EFFICIENCY

Written By:
Stefano Smith

CHAMPIONSHIP FINANCES
An Imprint of CHAMPIONSHIP FINANCES, LLC
www.championshipfinances.com

© **Copyright 2024 - All rights reserved.**

The content contained within this book may not be reproduced, duplicated, or transmitted without direct written permission from the author or the publisher. This book is a product of Championship Finances, LLC.

First Edition **ISBN**: 979-8-9890584-1-9

Legal Notice:
This book is copyright protected. It is only for personal use. You cannot amend, distribute, sell, use, quote or paraphrase any part, or the content within this book, without the consent of the author or publisher. Under no circumstances will any blame or legal responsibility be held against the publisher, or author, for any damages, reparation, or monetary loss due to the information contained within this book, either directly or indirectly.

Disclaimer:
Please note the information contained within this document is for educational and entertainment purposes only. All effort has been executed to present accurate, up to date, reliable, complete information. No warranties of any kind are declared or implied. Readers acknowledge that the author is not engaged in the rendering of legal, financial, medical, or professional advice. The content within this book has been derived from various sources. Please consult a licensed professional before attempting any techniques outlined in this book. By reading this document, the reader agrees that under no circumstances is the author responsible for any losses, direct or indirect, that are incurred as a result of the use of the information contained within this document, including, but not limited to, errors, omissions, or inaccuracies.

Fair use title: 17 U.S. Code Section 107 of the Copyright Act 1976 protects quotes, images, and comments used in this book.

Designed by CHAMPIONSHIP FINANCES, LLC

Library of Congress Cataloging-in-Publication Data available upon request.

1 2 3 4 5 6 7 8 9 10

Veteran Owned

⚠ WARNING

This book contains valuable information that can cause financial awareness and x-rays may show that dawg in you. Some readers may experience the sudden urge to create a budget, track expenses, and save money. This book can also cause readers to cut unnecessary cost and develop a resistance to payment shopping. **Side Effects Include:** increased bank account balance, heightened frugality, and financial stability. **Caution:** Learning about percentage-based budgets can make you financially responsible and dominate in all aspects of life. Results may vary.

You Have A Purpose.

WNBA

The Championship Trophy

"So many people contributed to my journey, it would be all too simple to deem my career a single effort. It is not. I'm the product of a village."

— **Tina Thompson**
4 x WNBA Champion

FIFA

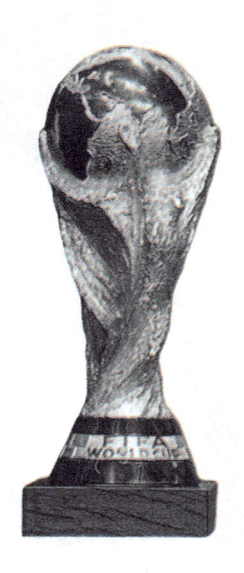

Coupe De Monde

"I start early, and I stay late, day after day, year after year. It took me 17 years and 114 days to become an over night success."

— Lionel Messi
2023 FIFA World Cup Champion

NHL

The Stanley Cup

"The day I stop giving is the day I stop receiving. The day I stop learning is the day I stop growing." — "You miss 100% of the shots you don't take."

**— Wayne Gretzky
4 x Stanley Cup Champion**

NBA

The Larry O'Brien Trophy

"If you're trying to achieve, there will be roadblocks. I've had them; everybody has had them. But obstacles don't have to stop you. If you run into a wall, don't turn around and give up. Figure out how to climb it, go through it, or work around it."

**— Michael Jordan
6 x NBA Champion**

US OPEN

The US Open Trophy

"Being strong is never easy. Not in this world we live in... Standing up for yourself is not going to be easy, but its eventually respected. Those are the people who've made a difference in this world, people that stand up for what's right. If you look at history, those are the people that you really remember."

— Serena Williams
23 Grand Slam Singles Titles

NFL

The Vince Lombardi Trophy

"I think sometimes in life the biggest challenges end up being the best things that happens in life." —"Things don't correct themselves, you've got to go out there and work hard to correct them."

**— Tom Brady
7 x NFL Super Bowl Champion**

F1

F1 World Drivers Championship Trophy

"As a driver, you've always got to believe in your heart that you've got what it takes to win it. You've always got to believe in yourself. You've always got to arrive on the day and believe it can happen. You've always have to believe in the positives."

**— Lewis Hamilton
11 x F1 World Drivers Champion**

MLB

The Commissioner's Trophy

"The longer you wait to decide what you want to do, the more time you're wasting. It's up to you to want something so badly that your passion shows through in your actions. Your actions, not your words, will do the shouting for you"

— Derek Jeter
5 x World Series Champion

PGA

The Wanamaker Trophy

"Days when you just don't have it, don't pack it in, you give it everything you got. You grind it out"

**— Tiger Woods
81 x PGA Tour Victories**

OLYMPICS

The Olympic Medal

"I like to just think of myself as a normal person who has a passion, has a goal and a dream and goes out and does it. And that's really how I've always lived my life."

— **Michael Phelps**
23 x Olympic Gold Medalist

WBC

The WBC Belt

"Im a professional World Champion. Of Course, If you're a World Champion, you're working harder than everybody else. You're making the commitment and you're making the sacrifices. If it were easy, everybody would be able to do it. Everybody would be able to be World Champion, but everybody can't be. Everybody doesn't have it in them."

— **Laila Ali**
WBC, WIBA, IWBF, IBA Womens
Super Middleweight Champion

TABLE OF CONTENTS

PAGE:

XXV — **Preface:**
Creating The Rules Of Financial Efficiency

01 — **Chapter 1: Budgeting:**
The 50/30/20 Budget Rule | True Budgeting Fundamentals | Front-End Budgeting | Back-End Budgeting | Signs Of Having To Much Debt | Improper Debt Structure | Proper Debt Structure | Percentage-Based Budgeting | Creating A Percentage-Based Budget | Bring It In

22 — **Chapter 2: Savings & Investing:**
Put You First! | Saving Through Automation | Reducing Financial Risk | Sinking Accounts | High Yield Savings Account | 20% Saving | Net Stat-Line | *Championship Mindset* | Just Make More Money | Understanding Ratio-Based Financing | Financial Awareness | The Secret Income Stream | The Gray Area Of Investing | Traditional Investments | Alternative Investments | Intellectual Property | Private Equity Investing

42 — **Chapter 3: Mortgages:**
MVP Terms | What Is A Mortgage | Mortgage Types Loans | The Home Buying Process | Qualifying | *Championship Mindset* | Affordability | The 28/36 Mortgage Rule Net Sat-Line | Nothing But Net | The Mortgage Salary Rule

TABLE OF CONTENTS >>>

PAGE: LOADING...

62   **Chapter 4: Mortgage Fundamentals:** Down Payment | Mortgage Term | Mortgage Interest | Cumulative Interest | The Affects Of Interest | Amortization Schedule | *Championship Mindset* | Early Mortgage Pay Off | Mortgage Extension | Home Equity Line Of Credit | House Hacking | The Efficiency Of Renting

88   **Chapter 5: Vehicles:** Vehicle Use Cases | The BIG 3 Of Vehicle Ownership | Too Much Vehicle | Vehicle Purchasing Range | The One Size Fits Most Vehicle Rule | The 20/4/10 Rule | *Championship Mindset* | Net Stat-Line | Other Ways To Reduce Vehicle Payments | Vehicle Leasing | The 1% Vehicle Lease Rule | Calculate A Lease Deal

114   **Chapter 6: Consumer Debt:** Secured Debt | Unsecured Debt | Revolving Credit-Debt | Installment Debt | Consumer Credit Spending | The 20/10 Rule | Net Stat-Line | The Benefit Of Credit Cards | *Championship Mindset* | Minimum Monthly Payment | The Double-Edge Sword | High Interest Debt | Credit Utilization

TABLE OF CONTENTS >>>

Download Complete...

PAGE:

132 **Chapter 7: Student Loans:** The Purpose Of Student Loans | The Different Types Of Student Loans | Federal Student Loans | Private Student Loans | The Student Loan Crisis | *Championship Mindset* | Borrowing With Salary In Mind | The Student Loan Rule | Net Stat-Line | Interest on Student Loans | Educational Savings Accounts | Maximize Your Student Loans | Alternative Education | Curving The Cost of College | Student Loan Repayment Terms | Student Loan Pay Off Strategies

156 END OF SEASON REVIEW

159 **Chapter 8: With Great [Credit] Comes Great Responsibility:** The FICO Credit Scoring System | Factors Determining Credit Score | Key Terms | The Credit Utilization Rule | The Vantage Credit Scoring System | Internal Ratings-Based Approach IRB | Business Credit Score | What Can Lower Your Credit Score | How To Improve Your Credit Score | Trade-line

174 **Chapter 9: The Most Important Stat:**

THE RULES:

Chapter 1 : The 50/30/20 Budget Rule . . . . Page 02

          *The Rules of Thumb . . . . Page 17

Chapter 2 : The 20% Savings Rule . . . . Page 26

Chapter 3 : The 28/36 Mortgage Rule . . . . Page 53

          The Mortgage Salary Rule . . . . Page 60

Chapter 4 : *Amortization Schedule . . . . Page 68

Chapter 5 : The "One Size fits Most" Vehicle Rule . . . . . Page 95

          The 20/4/10 Rule . . . . Page 96

          The 1% Vehicle Lease Rule . . . . Page 109

Chapter 6 : The 20/10 Credit-Debt Rule . . . . Page 118

Chapter 7 : The Student Loan Rule . . . . Page 139

Chapter 8 : The Credit Utilization Rule . . . . Page 162

THE NET STAT-LINE:

Chapter 2 : The Savings Net Stat-Line . . . . Page 27

Chapter 3 : The Mortgage Net Stat-Line . . . . Page 58

Chapter 5 : The Vehicle Net Stat-Line . . . . Page 106

Chapter 6 : The Credit-Debt Net Stat-Line . . . . Page 123

Chapter 7 : Student Loan Net Stat-Line . . . . Page 144

End Of Season STAT-LINE Review . . . . Page 156

Don't Quit.

PREFACE

Personal finance, for me, has always been a juggling act of earning, spending, investing, and saving. I've read many books, watched countless videos, and attended multiple seminars and even though my understanding of finances grew exponentially, somehow I struggle to find the right balance. The hole in my pocket was a real thing and I was determined to find the person, place, or thing that was robbing me of my hard earned money. They say *"personal finance is personal"* and that's exactly how I took it. In retrospect, I couldn't tell if it was taxes, inflation, or just poor money management because it seemed the more I earned, the less I had. And I was always pretty good at math, so I thought.

Then I questioned whether my investments were generating enough passive income to be deemed a success or should I pivot? It's said that the average millionaire has multiple streams of income and saves to invest 65% of it, which seemed like an impossible feat given I couldn't save 40% of my income if I tried. I also assumed saving would get easier as my income grew, but this was not the case. At a macro level, it seemed this issue was bigger than me after watching a CNBC segment that said nearly 50% of Americans earning $100k a year are living paycheck-to-paycheck. Determined to find answers, I set out to solve this problem.

While at a conference in BROOKLYN we decided to attend a Nets basketball game at the Barclays Center—which was several blocks from our hotel. On the tv in the clubroom, I overheard a sports analyst reviewing the stat-line of one Kevin Durant from a previous game. The analyst mentioned how efficient Durant was at scoring and how he barely needed the ball to affect the game. He scored 30 points on that night, taking only 13 shots, and had the ball in his hand for less than a minute for the entire game. It took me a minute to process what I just heard and thought, how ridiculously efficient it was for a basketball player to score 30 points in a 48 minute game while only having the ball in his hand for less than a minute. This meant, with the fewest possessions, he outscored everyone on the court.

The analyst went on to another stat-line called the *player efficiency rating* (PER). And listen, I watch sports, but rarely do I get into the weeds of analyzing. So, for those of you who are a "causal" fan hold on tight. PER is a *per-minute rating* scheme that sums a player's positive accomplishments versus the player's negative accomplishments and calculates a per-minute score of game time production, performance, and efficiency. For context, a good PER is 15, a great one is 20, and Kevin Durant had a PER of 32 that night.

After the game, I walked along the **BROOKLYN** pier adjacent to the hotel and wondered who were the most efficient athletes in and across all sports? And was there was a correlation between player efficiency and winning? Surely, the very nature golf is measured in efficiency that the greats like Tiger Woods learned to master at an early age. Then I turned to other efficiency ratings schemes like WARP, *wins above replacement player*, which the MLB and WNBA both use to measure the effect that one player has on the team's success when replaced by another player. This efficiency stat-line is what WNBA player Candace Parker excelled at and gained great recognition for during the playoffs. Most casual football fans have at least heard the acronym QBR, *quarterback efficiency rating*, which, you guessed it, measures the efficiency of quarterbacks. NFL quarterback Aaron Rogers dominated this stat-line throughout his entire career, becoming one of the most efficient quarterbacks in NFL history with a QBR of 103.6, with a young Patrick Mahomes quickly catching up.

Heading up to the hotel's rooftop terrace overlooking the BROOKLYN BRIDGE, it hit me in a stream of various theories. What if I was giving my money away before it got to me by financing too many "essential" living items? Was I only managing and investing what little money I had left? And why was it the more I made, the more expensive my lifestyle became?

As the wheel turned, I wondered if the same principals of player performance analytics used in professional sports could be applied to personal finance? If so, what information would I need to analyze my own financial performance and efficiency? I knew it had to be percentage-based if I wanted to save and invest 65% of my income like the average millionaire. Additionally, I had to determine which debts and expenses were negatively affecting my budget in order to optimize my income. This led me to some of the most commonly accepted "rules of thumb" for budgeting in *personal finance* and included rules like *the 50/30/20 budget rule, the 28/36 mortgage rule*, and *the 20/4/10 rule*. It may seem like jiberesh for now but you will understand by the end of this reading.

I found that financial experts universally agreed on the principals of these rules to keep consumers from taking on too much debt and becoming over-leveraged. The more I followed these rules, the more efficient I became and suddenly the path to positive *net* cash flow, investing, and financial freedom was clear. It

PREFACE

would appear I've found the base for *The Rules of Financial Efficiency*, but of course it couldn't be that simple. The problem was each debt category has its own rule of thumb which was not designed to work with one another. For instance, the mortgage rule helps individuals figure out how much house they can afford, but doesn't consider the rules of thumb for vehicle loans, student loans, or consumer credit-debt. Then, some rules use *gross* income and others use *net* income, which will prove problematic when trying to calculate a financially efficient budget.

I discovered at the core of the rules of thumb, they were blueprints on how to create a **PERCENTAGE-BASED BUDGET**, but it was missing something. This forced me to draw from other finance and accounting principles such as *debt-to-income ratios*, *zero-based budgets* (ZBB), and *cash flow statements* to make it applicable. That's when it clicked, to combine the rules of thumb and the finance principles to create a **PERCENTAGE-BASED BUDGET STAT-LINE!** This allowed me to combine **ALL** the rules and see what debts were consuming the largest portions of my income. Then by reducing those percentages, I could save and invest more efficiently. And as the financial world focused on earning more money, I focused on preserving the cash I already had to make other investments. Reflecting on a quote from Cornelius Vanderbilt, *"Any fool can make a fortune, but it takes a man with brains to hold on to it."*

The challenge was to simplify the concept enough for young adults to understand the benefits of creating a *percentage-based budget*, but detailed enough to captivate seasoned adults with financial woes. Let's face it, personal finance is not too exciting and if it sounds like a nightmare writing this book, trust me, at least you get to read the finished product.

After years of research, *The Rules of Financial Efficiency* was born. This book aims to breakdown the most commonly accepted rules of thumb to create a percentage-based budget—helping readers achieve financially efficiency. Championship Finances: *The Rules of Financial Efficiency* introduces new and familiar concepts to help set the foundation for the next generation of financial athletes. With the younger generation embracing a new era of limitless financial opportunities from tech and A.I. to investments and entrepreneurship, it seems they have their sights set on escaping the first rule of thumb, *the 40/40/40 rule.*

The 40/40/40 Rule

"Work 40 hours a week, for 40 years, and live off 40% of savings."

Personal finance is highly subjective, and there's no one right way to invest or spend your money; however, there are some fundamental truths that apply. So, as you may not agree with all the content in this reading, use the concepts as a general guide to challenge the way you think about personal finance. As you read, follow along to create your own percentage-based budget and consider that everyone's debts, expenses, and circumstances won't be the same. Last, fact check everything!

"Maybe its good we don't know what will happen next in our stories, because if we did, we might not turn the page. Or we might skip ahead and never experience the good that comes out of the hard moments we're living through."
— Simone Biles

"Crown"

Always Believe.

1

BUDGETING

Budgeting is the playbook for your finances; if you don't follow it, you're going to fumble the bag.

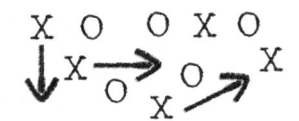

When it comes to budgeting, staying ahead of the game is a crucial part of financial efficiency. However, creating a game plan and building a budget seems to be the most overlooked step in personal finance. Creating a budget puts you one step ahead of the 70% of Americans who don't take this critical step for their finances. Most of us never learned how to budget properly from either our parents or the education system. The extent of our knowledge on saving and budgeting is the piggy bank we got as children. However, making a budget is essential because *a budget is the instructions for your income.*

There are many methods of budgeting and saving, one of which is called the *budget envelope.* This entails labeling multiple envelopes with different debt and expense categories and inserting the exact amount of cash in each envelope—praying not to run out of money by the end of the month. For some individuals, seeing the money in physical form helps establish an emotional connection to what they pay out each month. Another strategy is using a physical budget-planner, notebook, or excel spreadsheet. Nowadays, most budget planners are online or app-based and here are a few platforms to better manage your spending habits such as: *mint.intuit.com*, *rocketmoney.com*, or *youneedabudget.com*. No matter how you decide to budget, you need a system, and one of the most popular systems is the first rule of thumb—*the 50/30/20 budget rule*.

The 50/30/20 Budget Rule

"Allocate 50% of the monthly net income for needs, 30% for wants, and 20% for savings."

The 50/30/20 budget rule is a tool that gives consumers an easy way to budget their income each pay period. Each number represents the percentage of NEEDS, WANTS, and SAVINGS that consumes the monthly *net* income. While this rule is applicable to roughly 95% of earners, our calculations are based on the median annual *gross* income in the US of $45,000.

50%
"Allocate 50% of the monthly net income for needs…"

This portion of the rule suggests to allocate 50% of your monthly *net* income for NEEDS, such as debts, expenses, and essential living items. This includes housing, utilities, childcare, vehicle payments, and other essentials like groceries, fuel, and pet care.

For our first example, calculate 50% for needs using $2,925 to represent the monthly *net* income, then multiply by 50%. The score reflects the most you should spend on needs.

Multiply: $2,925 monthly net income x 50% needs
Score: = $1,462.50 needs

CHAPTER ONE

30%
"Allocate 30% of the monthly net income for wants…"

Next, this portion of the rule suggests allocating 30% of your monthly *net* income for **WANTS**. This could be shopping, movie night with friends and family, daily coffee, etc. The 30% seems like a lot for personal consumption, but let's expand the list of wants. Within the 30%, we must include hobbies, birthdays, holidays, anniversaries, and vacations just to name a few.

For the next example, calculate 30% for wants using $2,925 to represent the monthly *net* income, then multiply by 30%. The score reflects the most we should spend on wants.

Multiply: $2,925 monthly net income x 30% wants
Score: = $877.50 wants

CAME UP! THAT'S ALL ME!

20%
"Allocate 20% of the monthly net income for savings…"

Last, we have 20% for **SAVINGS**. The 20% savings can be slightly misleading because of all the different ways to save. Not only personal savings but *traditional investments* such as Roth IRAs, 401(k)s, retirement savings, bonds, mutual and index funds are all included in the 20% savings.

Calculate 20% for savings using $2,925 to represent the monthly *net* income, then multiply by 20%.

Multiply: $2,925 monthly net income x 20% savings
Score: = $585 savings

The 50/30/20 budget rule is a solid guide, but it's important to remember that everyone's financial situation is unique and may require different needs. As previously stated, this rule is applicable to nearly 95% of earners in the US, therefore, it would be impractical for an individual earning in the top 1%, or $650k+, to spend 50% of their income on needs. So, looking at the order of needs, wants, and savings, this ratio could be arrange to 40/20/40, respectively, and if you're EXTREMELY financially efficient—30/20/50. (see income chart on page 26)

As the complexity of your financials evolve, you will need to gather more advanced tools for budgeting your income. Managing investment portfolios, real estate, 401(k) retirement accounts, 529 plan accounts, IRAs, life insurance, estate planning, and joint spousal accounts will take a great deal of effort to map out beyond *the 50/30/20 budget rule*. Also, establishing a system of checks and balances to keep both parties on track will be key and you should seek to work with a *Certified Financial Planner* (CFP) or *Certified Financial Advisor* (CFA) to help you achieve your financial goals.

OK, NOW THE GOOD STUFF!

True Budgeting Fundamentals

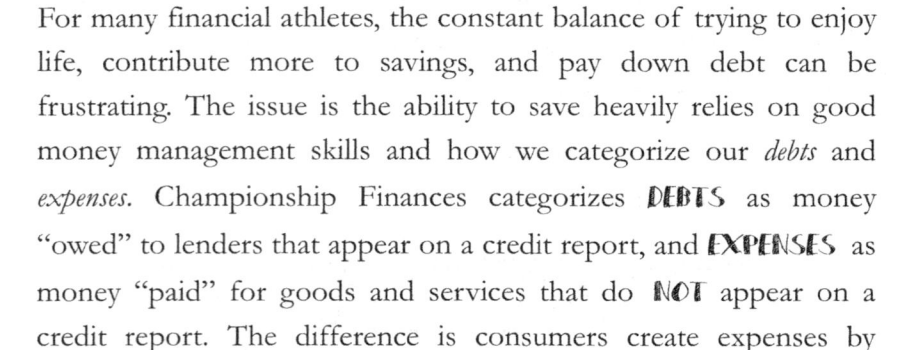

For many financial athletes, the constant balance of trying to enjoy life, contribute more to savings, and pay down debt can be frustrating. The issue is the ability to save heavily relies on good money management skills and how we categorize our *debts* and *expenses*. Championship Finances categorizes DEBTS as money "owed" to lenders that appear on a credit report, and EXPENSES as money "paid" for goods and services that do NOT appear on a credit report. The difference is consumers create expenses by purchasing goods and services but create debts by borrowing money. For example, you wouldn't finance an energy bill, because it's an expense.

There are two types of expenses, *fixed expenses* which are expenses for essential living items and *variable expenses* which vary by consumer. *Debts* are <u>credit reported</u> financed items attached to monthly payments. For a list of credit reported debts and non-credit reported expenses, review the tables below.

Credit Reported Debts: (included but not limited to)

Housing	Car Payments	Second Mortgages
Credit Cards	Motorcycles	Construction Loans
Student Loans	Store Cards	Co-Signed Loans
Personal Loans	Financed Recreation Vehicles	Tax Installment Agreements
Lines Of Credits	Financed Furniture	Collections
Home Equity Lines Of Credits	Joint Loans	Government Mandated Payments

From the <u>credit reported</u> *debt* table, we see these items are subject to appear on a credit report. Consumers have *indirect control* over the debt payments once the debt is acquired, therefore, classifying "debts" as *back-end* budget items.

Non-Credit Reported Fixed Expenses: (included but not limited to)

Homeowner's Insurance	Fuel	Day Care
Auto Insurance	Utilities	Taxes
Life Insurance	Groceries	Internet
Health Insurance	Alimony	Child Support
Home Owners Association HOA	Cell Phone Service	Savings

From the <u>non-credit reported</u> *fixed expense* table, we see these items are mostly non-negotiable expenses and are usually **NOT** subject to appear on a credit report. Consumers have more control over fixed expenses than debt because it's based on lifestyle choice and personal consumption. For this reason, "fixed expenses" are classified as *front-end* budget items.

**DEBT = CREDIT REPORT,
EXPENSES = NO CREDIT REPORT**

Non-Credit Reported Variable Expenses: (included but not limited to)

Subscription Services	Giving	Cable
Entertainment	Takeout	Hobbies
Grooming (Hair, Nails)	Pet Care	Gym Memberships
Private School	Lawn Care	Parking / Tolls

From the <u>non-credit reported</u> *variable expense* table, we see these items are mostly goods and services that do **NOT** appear on a credit report. Consumers usually have *direct control* over "variable expenses," so they also classify as *front-end* budget items.

Front-End Budgeting

Good money management is an important skill-set to have because it reflects how you, the consumer, budget your income. There are two categories we use when discussing *true* budgeting: *front-end* and *back-end*. Front-end budget items consists of fixed and variable expenses that the consumer mostly controls. It's up to the consumer to decide whether to choose a more affordable cable and internet package, mow their own lawn, or how much Starbucks they consume. The consumer's lifestyle choice dictates the demand for goods and services and in these examples, the consumer has *direct control* of how the income is spent. This makes fixed and variable expenses classify as *front-end budget items*.

You had me at Starbucks...

A savings plan built on front-end budgeting usually won't last long because it does not solve the underlying issue. Many consumers spend frivolously and stop short of what's needed for essential living items like food, water, and shelter to name a few.

Cellphones Are Essentials Bro!

Many consumers believe cutting out daily expenditures will help solve their spending problems. Spending less on goods and services like takeout, streaming subscriptions, and gym memberships is the go-to for most financial gurus, but let's see what's happening in the background with *back-end budgeting*.

Back-End Budgeting

It's about to Get Real!

Back-end budgeting consist of structured debt payments items and are the biggest "income eaters" in personal finances. The reason is most consumers are **PAYMENT BUYERS**—meaning they shop for monthly **PAYMENTS** rather than **PRICE**. This makes smart back-end budgeting the foundation of financial efficiency. **Contrary to common belief, it is not the consumer who dictates how the money is spent, but rather the debt they acquire.* The amount of money remaining each month depends on how efficient you where when adding structured debt payments to the monthly *net* income. This is because the consumer controls the remaining income after the debt obligations are satisfied—hence, *indirect control*. It's an easier decision to skip a *variable expense* like Starbucks than it is to skip a monthly structured *debt* like a car payment. This is the key difference between *front-end* and *back-end* budget items. Of course, nothing is final, and there are ways to refinance or restructure your debt.

Consumers can gain better control of their income, but the game plan for tackling debt is just as essential as the amount of debt they finance or borrow. Many consumers "over-finance" their monthly *net* income with monthly *debt* payments until there's nothing left to save. **LARGE** debts, such as *mortgages, vehicle loans,* and *student loans,* produce **LARGE** payments that consume a **LARGER** percentage of the monthly *net* income. This may sound redundant, but when consumers add new debts, a greater portion of their monthly earnings goes toward *servicing debt*—or making payments. This also works in reverse. When consumers eliminate debt, more of their monthly earnings is available for savings and investments.

The **NET** of it is, all we have is 100% of our monthly *net* income, and if we finance 90% of it away on back-end debt items, what's left is 10% for front-end expenses. More on this later.

TALK THAT TALK!
The key to proper back-end debt structure is creating a *percentage-based budget.* While **The 50/30/20 Budget Rule** is a good example of a percentage-based budget, the *Net Stat-line* goes a few steps beyond that. It assigns a percentage to each debt item to help you determine how much debt to take on. As you read, we will discuss the "rules of thumb" recommended for each debt category.

Interest
Interest on debt also affects the monthly debt payments. High-interest on essential living items is extremely inefficient and can significantly increase your monthly payments. Therefore, it's important to structure your *percentage-based budget* on these three principles: *necessity, monthly net income,* and *interest* applied.

INTEREST-TING....!

CHAPTER ONE

Water Break...

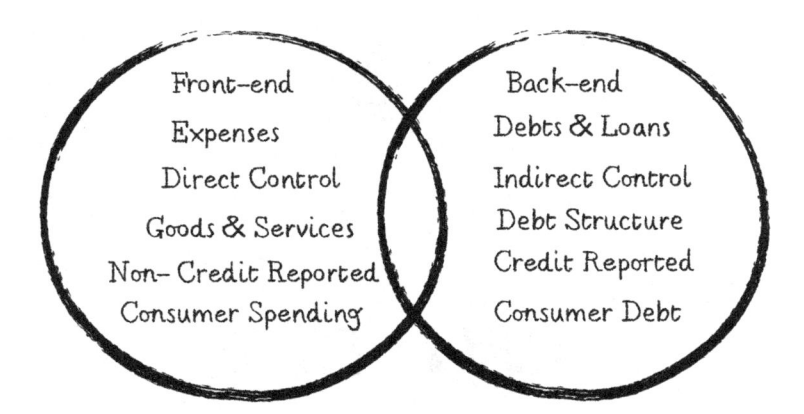

Left circle:
Front-end
Expenses
Direct Control
Goods & Services
Non-Credit Reported
Consumer Spending

Right circle:
Back-end
Debts & Loans
Indirect Control
Debt Structure
Credit Reported
Consumer Debt

Signs Of Having Too Much Debt

Being buried in debt can be an uncomfortable feeling for anyone. Unfortunately, financed debt can take years to repay—leaving borrowers feeling helpless. If you've tried every method to reduce spending and still live paycheck-to-paycheck, chances are you have too much debt. For instance, if your mortgage payment or rent is too expensive for your current finances, it does not matter how many nights of the week you avoid ordering takeout, it will not change the fact that your house is too expensive. When your debt payments are too high and there's just enough money or not enough money to cover the payments, you are *over-leveraged*—meaning unable to meet your debt payment obligations due to lack of income. Here are a few signs that you might be over-leveraged:

- debt balances remain the same each month
- relying on credit cards for simple purchases
- living paycheck-to-paycheck
- unable to establish a retirement account
- unable to establish an emergency savings fund

Can't Keep a Real one Down...

HALF-TIME

Faith...Patience...Determination

"I'm very different than your parents because your parents don't want you to fail and be uncomfortable. I love you enough to allow you to fail."
— Dawn Staley

CHAPTER ONE

Improper Debt Structure

Now that we've set our basis for knowing the difference between *front-end* and *back-end* budgeting, let's look at what causes improper debt structure. The three primary causes are the lack of financial education; structuring debts based on *gross* income; and failing to create a percentage-based budget. Financial education is why you are here, but what makes structuring debt on *gross* income financially "unwise?" To explain, let's start with understanding what a debt-to-income ratios (DTI).

Debt-to-Income Ratio (DTI)
In finance, there is a relationship between a consumers monthly *gross* income and their monthly debt payments. This relationship is displayed as a "ratio" between the two. The balancing act of increasing one's income while adding or subtracting debt makes this ratio ever changing. This is known as the *debt-to-income ratio* (DTI).

MVP Terms:
- A debt-to-income ratio identifies what portion of an individual's monthly GROSS income is being used to repay debts and displays it as a percentage.

Example:

If an individual (A) earns $1,000 a month but pays $1,000 a month towards debt payments, they've effectively spent 100% of their income; therefore, their *debt-to-income* ratio would be 100%. If individual (B) earns $1,000 a month pays $500 or half of their income towards debt payments, then their *debt-to-income* ratio would be 50%. A good DTI, in personal finance, is roughly 36% or lower. This percentage will depend on how strategic you are when structuring and acquiring debt.

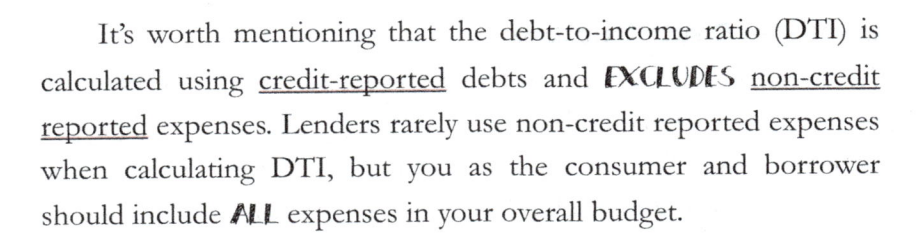

It's worth mentioning that the debt-to-income ratio (DTI) is calculated using <u>credit-reported</u> debts and **EXCLUDES** <u>non-credit reported</u> expenses. Lenders rarely use non-credit reported expenses when calculating DTI, but you as the consumer and borrower should include **ALL** expenses in your overall budget.

Find The Debt-To-Income Ratio (DTI):

For this example, use $1,350 to represent the sum of the individual's monthly *debt* payments and $3,750 to represent the individual's monthly *gross* income.

Calculate the monthly DTI by dividing the monthly debt payments by the monthly *gross* income. Then multiply by 100 to find the percentage.

Divide: $1,350 debt payments ÷ $3,750 monthly gross income
Multiply: = 0.36 x 100
Score: = 36% DTI

From the example above, this individual has a debt-to-income ratio of 36%. The key factor to remember is that debt-to-income (DTI) uses <u>*gross*</u> income to calculate this ratio, not <u>*net*</u> income.

Debt-to-Net Income Ratio (DTNI)
On the other hand, a *debt-to-[net] income ratio* is calculated the same way, but uses **NET** income instead of *gross* income. *Net income* is earned income or profit after tax deductions. More on this later.

NOTHING BUT NET!

Find The Debt-To-Net Income Ratio (DTNI):

For this example, use $1,350 to represent the sum of the monthly *debt* payments and $2,925 to represent the monthly *net* income.

Calculate the monthly debt-to-[*net*] income ratio (DTNI) by dividing the monthly *debt* payments by the monthly *net* income. Then multiply by 100 to find the percentage.

Divide: $1,350 debt payments ÷ $2,925 monthly net income
Multiply: = 0.46 x 100
Score: = 46% DTNI

Reviewing both examples, we see using *net* income tells a different story than *gross* income. A 10% difference may seem insignificant, but it's a **BIG** deal in the world of financial efficiency when every percentage point matters.

ALL OFFENSE, NO DEFENSE...

Why Not Gross Income?

When creating a budget, it's important to use the most accurate numbers possible. When we get paid, most of us look at the *net* earnings—maybe look at what came out in taxes and go about our day. But rarely do we consider the *gross* as real income. When we cash our checks at the bank, we don't expect to get the pre-taxed *gross* amount back, nor do we expect to spend the pre-taxed *gross* amount at the grocery store. Let's define *gross*.

- Gross income is earned income or profit BEFORE deductions are subtracted, such as federal tax, state tax, Medicare, and social security.

Lenders and banks use *gross* income differently than we do. Lenders can and will lend you, the borrower, money based on how much you *gross* monthly or annually. We experience this when we purchase homes, vehicles, or apply for new credit cards. Using *gross* income isn't all bad, but borrowers can run into issues when using *gross* to create a *percentage-based budget*.

(Story Time...)

Here is another example of how gross income can be misleading. After earning an annual salary of $36.9 million, a **BROOKLYN NETS** basketball player paid $13.6 million in federal tax deductions, equating to a federal tax rate of 37%. Then the player paid another $4.02 million in state tax, $875k in FICA, $1.43 million in local tax, and $1.1 million in jock tax—*a tax that requires professional athletes to pay income tax in each state where they earn income from competing in games*. These tax deductions combined for $21.06 million, resulting in a whopping 57% of the player's annual *gross* salary—leaving a *net* or *take-home* income of $15.87 million.

Nasty Work!

Subtract: $36.9 million gross salary − $21.06 million total taxes

Score: = $15.87 million net income

Granted, **NEW YORK** has some of the highest tax rates, and surely the player is receiving significant tax benefits, but in this scenario, more than half of the player's salary went to taxes. This still doesn't include the cost for managers, agents, accountants, and lawyers, etc.

That's Gross...

Proper Debt Structure

When we talk about budgeting, it's important to establish our *percentage-based budget* on *net* or *take-home* income. The reason we build the budget on *net* income is because it better represents what we actually have to spend. Using *net* income to create a percentage-based budget will help you decide when to take on more debt and how much debt to take on.

So, Gross is the Juice, But Net is the Sauce! IYKYK

CHAPTER ONE

- Net income or take-home income is earned income or profit AFTER deductions are subtracted, such as federal tax, state tax, Medicare and social security.

Think of *net* income as the financial anchor for your budget, but understand that most lenders use *gross* income to structure loans.

30-Second Time-Out...

For clarification, the term *household income* is the total income of every financially contributing member of the family over 15 years old. Household income is often used loosely with *net* or *take-home* income, but based on its definition, it does not apply to this conversation.

Back In!

Finally!

Percentage-Based Budgeting

A *percentage-based budget* is the crossroad between debt structure, *net* income, and the rules of thumb. *The goal of a percentage-based budget is to IDENTIFY the biggest portion of monthly net income and ORGANIZE your finances.* Creating a percentage-based budget means allocating a certain percent of your monthly *net* income to each debt category. Referring to **The 50/30/20 Budget Rule**, the 50% for NEEDS encapsulates the various debt categories such as housing, vehicle, student loans, etc; however, to "properly" create a percentage-based budget, you must itemize each debt category by percentage within the 50% portion of this rule. (further explained on page 17)

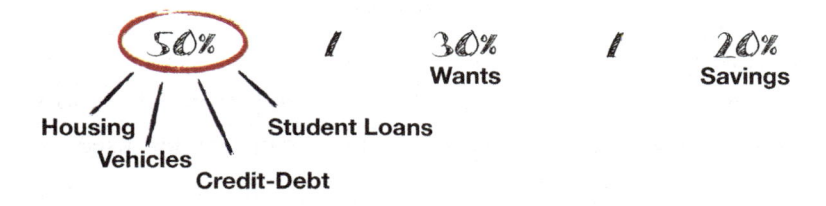

50% / 30% / 20%
Housing   Wants   Savings
Vehicles   Student Loans
           Credit-Debt

Creating A Percentage-Based Budget

Now, let's create a percentage-based budget using the rules of thumb, but first start by finding the monthly *net* income.

For simplicity, use the median annual *gross* income of a single individual earning $45,000 annually at a 22% federal tax rate. We did **NOT** include State tax, Medicare, Social Security, marital status, exemptions, and income tax brackets when calculating *net* income.

Step 1: Annual Federal Tax
Calculate the federal income tax deductions by multiplying the annual *gross* income of $45,000 by the federal tax rate of 22%.

Multiply: $45,000 annual gross income x 22% federal tax rate
Score: = $9,900 annual federal tax

Step 2: Annual Net Income
Subtract the annual federal tax amount from the annual *gross* income. This will give the annual *net* income.

Subtract: $45,000 annual gross income – $9,900 federal tax
Score: = $35,100 annual net income

Step 3: Monthly Net Income
Calculate the monthly *net* income by dividing the annual *net* income by 12 months.

Divide: $35,100 annual net income ÷ 12 months
Score: = $2,925 monthly net income

Step 4: Review The Rules of Thumb Stat-Line
As mentioned, the *rules of thumb* are derived from the most commonly accepted percentage-based budgeting guides used in finance and The Rule of Thumb Monthly Stat-Line represents the **BENCHMARK!** for what monthly debt payments should be.

CHAPTER ONE

Rules of Thumb
Monthly Stat-Line

Front-End
Fixed & Variable

Savings	Housing	Vehicle Payments	Credit-Debt	Student Loans	F/V Expenses
20%	28%	10%	10%	15%	17%

100%
Monthly Net Income

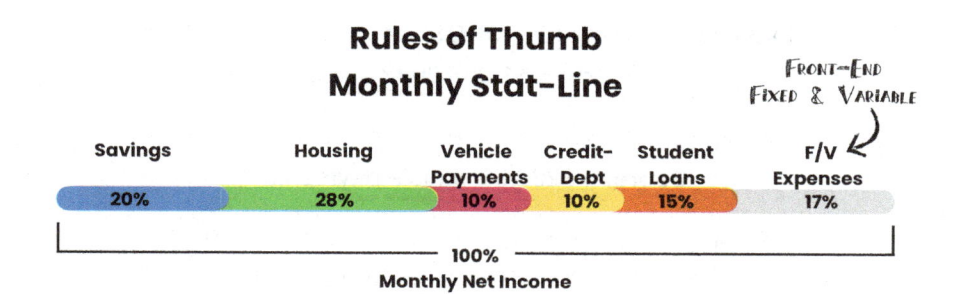

The Rules of Thumb Stat-Line is the benchmark for monthly debt payments and applies the recommended percentages to 100% of the monthly *net* income—creating a percentage-based budget. Each chapter explains the rule of thumb for each debt category.

The percentages for **Housing**, **Vehicle Payments**, **Credit/Debt**, and **Student Loans** are all structured debt payments subtracted from the monthly *net* income. If you recall, structured debt payments are classified as *back-end budget* items, while fixed and variable expenses (**F/V**) are *front-end budget* items. The savings category is unique because there's no money loss; however, it's still treated like a fixed expense, as it is a payment towards future debts and expenses in retirement.

Step 5: Percentage-Based Budget Calculations

Calculate the percentage-based budget using $2,925 to represent the monthly *net* income and multiply by the suggested percentages from the rules of thumb.

Multiply: $2,925 monthly net income x 20% or 0.20
Score: = $585 savings

Note: Use $3,750 as the monthly GROSS income when applying the housing rule. (see chapter 3 for details)

Multiply: $3,750 monthly **GROSS** income x 28% or 0.28
Score: = $1,050.00 housing

Multiply: $2,925 monthly net income x 10% or 0.10
Score: = $292.50 vehicle payments

Multiply: $2,925 monthly net income x 10% or 0.10
Score: = $292.50 credit-debt payments

Multiply: $2,925 monthly net income x 15% or 0.15
Score: = $438.75 student loan payments

Debt-To-Net Income (DTNI):

Monthly Net Income	→ $2,925.00
*Housing 28%	($1,050.00)
Vehicle Payment 10%	($292.50)
Credit & Debt Payments 10%	($292.50)
Student Loan Payments 15%	($438.75)
Total Monthly Debt Payments	**($2,073.75)** ←

+

Savings 20% (Fixed Expense)	(585.00)

Note: Savings will NOT be used in this example; Keep savings in the "dugout" until Chapter 2.

★ Final Step: Debt-To-Net Income Ratio

Calculate the debt-to-net income ratio (DTNI) by dividing the total monthly debt payments by the monthly *net* income. Then multiply by 100 to find the percentage.

Divide: $2,073.75 total debt payments ÷ $2,925 monthly *net* income
Multiply: = 0.70 x 100
Final Score: = 70% DTNI

CHAPTER ONE

Remember, **The 50/30/20 Budget Rule** states to allocate 50% of the income to needs, in this case, it's the total monthly debt payments. The total monthly debt payments from our example is $2,073.75 which gives us a total *debt-to-net income ratio* of 70%. This example shows how quickly debt payments can consume the monthly *net* income. A consistent game plan when acquiring debt will prove useful when trying to remain financially efficient.

See the Plan, Be the Plan...

Now let's calculate the remaining cash available. For this, subtract the debt-to-net income ratio of 70% from 100% of the monthly *net* income to get the available cash.

Subtract: 100% net income – 70% DTNI
Score: = 30% available cash

Cash Flow
Out of the 100% of *net* cash that flows into the account, 70% flows back out to debt payments, leaving 30% in the account. This is what's referred to as *cash flow*.

- Cash flow is the total amount of cash that flows into your account versus the total amount of cash that flows out.

The remaining 30%, or $877.50, of free cash is positive *net* cash flow, however we still have savings, investments, and other expenses. The objective of the "*GAME*" is to have more cash flowing in than out. The most efficient way to achieve this is to preserve the cash you have and use it to create more cash flow.

Aww Smart! Use the Cash Flow To make More Cash Flow

It's just a game. Learn how it works and play to win!

W-MANS!

Discretionary Income

If all debts, expenses, and essential living items are paid, you are free to do what you will with the remaining income because it is *discretionary income*. This is where the 30% for **WANTS** live.

- Discretionary income is the remaining amount of an individual's net income after tax deductions, debt and expense payments, savings, and essential items such as food, shelter, and clothing.

Bring It In

The point of a percentage-based budget is to have a clear picture of what debts and expenses are being taken out of your monthly *net* income. By seeing a percentage breakdown of each debt and expense category you can easily determine what is affecting you the most and what can be reduced or eliminated from your budget. This is how you become financially efficient.

Throughout each chapter, we will build a Championship Finances Net Stat-Line based on each rule of thumb—using the monthly *net* income. Last, we'll wrap up with an End of Season Review—analyzing how the Championship Finances Net Stat-Line compares to the Rules of Thumb Stat-line. The goal is to remain within 100% of our monthly *net* income while we work through each rule of thumb.

ASKING FOR A FRIEND BRO
THIS A MATH BOOK?

"If you are afraid of failure... you don't deserve to be successful."
— Charles Barkley

Notes

Chapter 1 Takeaways:
- A budget is the instructions for your income
- Debt-to-income ratio is the percentage of debt to gross income
- Debt-to-net income ratio is the percentage of debt to net income
- Percentage-Based Budgets help financial athletes identify what debts consume the most of their net income

SAVINGS & INVESTMENTS

Goalkeepers save goals, I save money; guess we both got our nets to protect. #BigSavingsEnergy

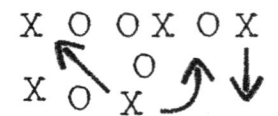

```
X  O  OX  O X
 ↖    O    ↗ ↓
X  O  X
    O  X
```

One of the most common misconceptions in personal finance is that you save what's left after paying debts and expenses. In actuality, it's quite the opposite. You may have heard the phrase *"pay yourself first,"*—meaning the first payment should always be to your personal savings goals when receiving your paycheck. Saving is a unique skill set that needs to be sharpened daily, and how well you manage your savings will determine how much you can invest. We all know it's easier said than done, but saving is the gateway to investment opportunities, so it's worth giving it everything you got.

I Got to Put Me First!

Learning to save is like learning the fundamentals of a sport. Once you create a percentage-based budget and practice the concept of *"paying yourself first,"* saving gets easier. It's suggested from the 50/30/20 budget rule to save at least 20% of your *net* or take-home income. As previously mentioned, savings can include *traditional investments* such as stocks, bonds, and cash or other investments like 401(k)s, traditional IRAs, Roth IRAs, 529 accounts, employee stock ownership plans (ESPOP), and *health savings accounts* (HSA), etc. Employer match 401(k)s come highly recommended by most financial experts because they are one of the most efficient ways to save. Employees benefit in two ways from these accounts. First, the employer matches the employees' contributions up to a certain percentage, making each contribution an <u>instant 100% return</u>. Second, it lowers the employees' *adjusted gross income* (AGI), resulting in lower income tax for the employee.

Saving Through Automation

You should structure your savings through automation as if it were paying a bill. Use your bank's transfer feature to set up a 20% withdrawal each pay period to your savings and retirement accounts. By achieving this, the rest of your debts, expenses, and financial decisions will fall into place. When beginning your savings journey, aim to achieve:

- a realistic percentage-based budget
- paying yourself first each pay period
- having a savings target weekly, monthly, and annually
- automating 20% of your net income to savings
- establishing an emergency savings fund

Let 'em Cook!

Reducing Financial Risk

As we've all experienced in recent years, emergency savings have become crucial to our well-being during uncertain times. It's reported that 70% of Americans do not have an emergency savings account. It takes a great deal of foresight to establish an emergency savings account, especially in good times; as some would say, *"save for a rainy day."* Saving three to six months' worth of debt and expense payments is standard, but due to inflation and other external factors, we see a "financial comfort zone" leaning towards six months for an emergency savings fund.

Having health and life insurance are other ways to reduce financial risk. Unpaid medical bills account for 66% of consumer bankruptcies in the U.S. and having the proper insurance can help protect you and your loved ones against significant financial loss. Life insurance is another way to reduce financial risk and protect your family's legacy. This highlights the importance of *estate planning* —which is creating a game plan, while living, on what happens to your assets when you pass. **(estate planning further explained on page 40)**

Sinking Accounts

Facts!

Does your head hurt yet? Imagine in a perfect world, you've structured your debt properly and cured your latté obsession. Also, you've mastered financial efficiency and eliminated most of your debts. And you're crushing it by making consistent contributions to investment- and retirement accounts, with a fully funded emergency savings account. Now what? You can spend the money on whatever you'd like, that's why it's called *discretionary income*, or you can put the money into savings for other investments, but this is typically frowned upon. Putting money into a savings account is perceived negatively by most financial experts, because the caveat to money in savings is *inflation*—also known as the *"silent thief."*

MVP Terms:

The Smoothest Of Criminals!

- Inflation is the increase in prices and the fall in the consumer's purchasing power.

Many believe choosing an investment vehicle that outpaces the rate of inflation is better than letting your money devalue in a savings account. What they don't mention is most investors save with the intention of investing by creating a *sinking account*.

Dropping Dimes!

- Sinking accounts are funds set aside for a specific purpose. Deposits are made in a special savings account with the intention to repay debts, replace assets, or to make future acquisitions.

Most people, unknowingly, have *sinking accounts* and a few examples are Christmas savings, vacation funds, or a down payment for a house. These are all examples of sinking accounts created with the intention of spending what's saved at a specific time or when the account reaches a specific amount. Good money management skills and becoming *net* cash flow positive is the secret to saving a sinking account for investment opportunities. This shows the importance of financial efficiency.

My Account Sinks every month
I think I got one Already...

High Yield Savings Account (HYSA)

To keep your savings as efficient as possible, consider putting your money into a *high yield savings account* (HYSA). A HYSA will give a better interest return—or *annual percentage yield* (APY)—than a traditional savings account. An HYSA's annual percentage yield ranges from 1.00% to as high as 6.00% compared to the average *money market* or traditional savings account offering a 0.22% APY. High yield savings accounts will also help generate a bit of *passive income* and is great for *emergency savings*. Little is known about HYSAs even though some of the largest financial institutions offer them. Here are a few:

Not You With
The Assist!!!

Banks Offering HYSA: (included but not limited to)

Synchrony Bank	CITI BANK
American Express	Lightstream by Truist Bank
Barclays Banking	Marcus by Goldman Sachs
SOFI	Apple via Goldman Sachs

20% Savings

Going back to **The 50/30/20 Budget Rule**, 20% of your *net* or take-home income is allocated to savings. With that said, saving 20% is not *"a one size fits all"* and will not work for everyone. For example, if you get an endorsement, or *Name Image and Likeness* deal (NIL) worth millions, we hope that you would use discernment with this suggestion and save more than 20%.

In personal finance, a different set of rules apply at different income levels, that's why it's essential to know where you stand financially. It's impractical for a financial athlete in the top 1% of earners to follow the same *"MONEY-PRINT"* as an athlete in the lower 50% bracket of earners and vice versa. *For clarity, this book is a general guide for roughly 95% of earners in the U.S.* and serves as a foundational tool for the remaining 5%.

Top Percentile Of Individual Earners In The US:

Top 1%	$650,000 and Up
Top 5%	$225,000 — $649,000
Top 10%	$135,000 — $224,000
90% of Earners	$134,000 and Below

This chart shows the *"BALL PARK"* national average of top earners in the U.S.—which 90% earn $134,000 and below. With that, the top percentile of earners will vary by city and state. For example, a top 1% earner in Alabama may not be in the top 1% in New York.

Owe, There's Levels to This!

It's time to add our first stat to our percentage-based budget monthly *net* stat-line. Keep in mind, the savings category stands out because there are no financial losses involved; however, it's still categorizes as a fixed expense since it is a payment for future retirement, debts and expenses.

★ **Find The 20% Monthly Savings From Net Income:**
Calculate the monthly savings using $2,925 to represent the monthly *net* income, then multiply by 20%. The score will reflect how much we should keep for savings.

Multiply: $2,925 monthly net income x 20% savings
Final Score: = $585 monthly savings

Loading...

**Championship Finances
Monthly Net Stat-Line**

| Savings | Housing | Vehicle Payments | Credit-Debt | Student Loans | F/V Expenses |

20%

100%
Monthly Net Income

Congratulations! You made it to our first *net* stat; **Savings**! Now let's continue to "stat pad" our *net* stat-line using the rules of thumb in each chapter. Follow along with your own monthly debt payments to calculate your personal *net* stat-line!

Standin On' Bidness!

Championship Mindset

Just Make More Money?
Hustle culture has created a grind hard—*"sleep when you die"*—mentality, which most believe is the answer to having more money. Although hustling and grinding long hours can be lucrative, it can also lead to severe burnout and self-neglect—which research shows this doesn't necessarily lead to happiness or building more wealth. *The reason is many people believe they can out-earn or outpace poor money management and by prioritizing making more, you neglect the concept of spending less.* It's reported that nearly 50% of Americans earning $100,000 a year live paycheck-to-paycheck, leaving the median earning worker wondering, how is this possible? We found, it boils down to the questions we ask ourselves.

Like, How you Fumble the $100K Bag, my Boy?!

Not that Question…

"How much do I need to earn to stop living paycheck-to-paycheck?"
Versus
"How much do I need to earn, AND NOT SPEND, to stop living paycheck-to-paycheck?"

~~Work~~ Think Smarter not Harder!

Money management is based on two fundamental categories: *how much you earn* and *how much you keep*. It's important to understand that making more money isn't always the first solution when trying to build wealth, because making more money does not automatically make you more financially efficient. Seek to learn the fundamentals of money management before trading more time for money.

Understanding Ratio-Based Financing

Over-financing can pick apart your percentage-based budget. Lenders structure most of our debts in a way that keeps us continuously servicing debt. Whenever we make big purchases, we borrow or *finance* the money in the form of a loan attached to fees and interest.

- Financing is money borrowed from a lender, or bank, to purchase items the borrower cannot afford or not willing to pay for outright. This is done under a contractual agreement to be paid back with fees and interest over a set term—meaning over time. Payments on financed items are usually monthly or quarterly.

Lenders allow borrowers to finance essential and non-essential living items based on the borrowers monthly debt-to-income ratio by using *ratio-based financing*. Ratio-based financing allows qualified borrowers to increase their standard of living based on what they can pay in monthly payments versus what they gross monthly. In other words, because most borrowers are "PAYMENT BUYERS," what they *"qualify"* for in monthly payments is not what they can *"afford"* in cash.

Spend Less Than You Earn

As a financial athlete, you need to be aware of the economic term called the *income effect*.

- The income effect is the change in consumer demand for goods and services based on the change in the consumer's income.

It may seem cliché to say, *"the more you make, the more you spend,"* but it goes deeper. When there is a significant increase in *real income*, the *consumer's new purchasing power* opens the door for more opportunities. This can ignite change in the psychology of a person from a poverty-stricken mindset, to a mindset of abundance. There's nothing wrong with an abundant mindset, but if not careful, these new spending habits can lead to living above your means, and eventually, living the "high life" will lead to *lifestyle creep*.

- Lifestyle creep is a psychological phenomenon that occurs when increased discretionary income leads to increased discretionary spending.

As real income increases, consumers tend to experience lifestyle creep, which leads to financing more items through ratio-based financing. When this happens, consumers are at risk of maxing out their monthly *net* income—leaving them with little to save. Making more money and spending more money creates a 1:1 ratio; however, earning more money and spending less, or the same, can create a more financially efficient ratio conducive to saving.

Subtract: $50,000 earning — $40,000 spending
Score: = $10,000 saving

Subtract: $90,000 earning — $80,000 spending
Score: = $10,000 saving

The hallmark sign of lifestyle creep is when consumers "RATIONALIZE" personal spending as a "RIGHT", based on what they feel they deserve, instead of a personal "CHOICE." Percentage-based budgets can help consumers avoid lifestyle creep.

Don't Creep Bro!

(Story Time...)

It's said that when Chad "Ochocinco" Johnson played for the Cincinnati Bengals during his 11-season NFL career, he saved 80% of his earnings. In an effort to remain living below his means, Chad bought fake jewelry and lived at the Bengals stadium for the first 2 years of his NFL career. Some may find his choice extreme, but

CHAPTER   TWO

Chad was looking for every opportunity to save his money. As he says, "money always looks better coming in, than going out."

He Really Like That FR, FR!

The Secret Income Stream

As stated, the average millionaire has seven sources of income, which is typically a combination of *active* and *passive* income. On the road to multiple passive income streams, the first source of income is usually active income—*money earned from employment.* We know this because the average age of a millionaire is 49, most of whom got there through long-term investments. In addition, we believe there is a secret source of income undoubtedly all *high-net-worth individuals* (HNWI) have. This secret source of income shapes the way high-net-worth individuals think, earn, and invest. The secret is the ability to SAVE!

The Art is In the Saving!

It's simple, yet effective. *The ability to save is a skill that high-net-worth individuals mastered during their rise because they learned early on that their number one wealth building tool is their money.* And if earned wages was their first source of income, then the ability to save must be their second. Here we reference a quote attributed to Benjamin Franklin, *"A penny saved, is a penny earned."* Meaning, it is as useful to save the money you already have, as it is to earn more money.

Dat Way!
Earn > Save > Invest

"It's not what one person does. One person is going to be the star of the game. It might have been the guy, who got the guy over, who's the real star of the game."
— Ken Griffey Jr.

HALF-TIME

MAMBA MENTALITY

"I don't know if I can. I want to find out. I want to see. I'm going to do what I always do: I'm going to break it down to its smallest form, smallest detail, and go after it. Day by day, one day at a time."
— Kobe Bean Bryant

THE GRAY AREA OF INVESTMENTS

How you choose to invest your money can be one of the toughest decisions to make in personal finance. The endless sea of financial opportunities can make it nauseating for those seeking to convert their *active income* into *passive income*. Investing isn't as straightforward as online gurus makes it seem and can leave a sour taste for those who've suffered a financial loss in an investment. The arena for investing can be very GRAY, because there's no "ONE" investment that's perfect for everyone. Investments can be traditional, such as stocks, bonds, and cash, or alternative—meaning literally "EVERYTHING ELSE"—like antique vehicles, precious metals, hotels, start-up companies, private equity, and sports teams, etc. Not to mention the different types of investment opportunities individuals have at every income level. While this is NOT a book on investing, it's important to understand the fundamentals of investments to make the most of your money.

So, Traditional Investments = Stocks, Bonds, & Cash...
Alternative Investments = Everything Else

MVP Terms:
- Passive Income is money that you do NOT actively work for.
- Active Income is money earned in wages from a job or business profits that you actively participate in, i.e. working a JOB!

Give Every Dollar A Job
You may have also heard the phrase *"make your money work for you."* Well, by sending your dollar bills out into the world to make you money through traditional and alternative investments—makes money your first employee. Always prioritize making your money work for you to maximize both your time and money.

Traditional Investments

Comparatively, traditional investments are safer than alternative investments but aren't as glamorous. The goal of traditional investments is to build wealth over time, generate income passively, and/or retire comfortably. There are 3 types of traditional investments **STOCKS, BONDS,** and **CASH**. Stocks and bonds we understand, but you're probably wondering how to invest in cash? **ANSWER:** Putting cash into a *high yield savings account* (HYSA), money market account, *certificate deposit* (CD), and/ or *health savings account* (HSA), makes investing cash a traditional investment.

- Stocks are shares of publicly traded companies sold to investors in the stock market in exchange for becoming an owner or shareholder. The value of the investment is determined by the volatility or rise and fall of the companies stock price.

Traditional IRA's, Roth IRA's, 401(k)s, ESOPs, and 529 plans are accounts that buy and sell *securities*—thus are classified as traditional investments. **(529 plan account explained on page 143)**

- IRA – Individual Retirement Account

- Employee Stock Ownership Plan (ESOP) gives employees stock in the company they work for—usually based on the length of their employment. (Not all companies offer this plan.)

- Bonds are loans to the government or a company at a fixed rate of return (RoR). In this scenario, the consumer is the lender.

The Difference Between Stocks & Bonds

Owning shares means you own a part of a company and owning bonds means you own part of the debt of a company. With bonds, there is less risk of losing money because it's earned at a fixed *annual percentage yield* (APY). For example, if you own a bond at a 6% APY and the company's stock "hypothetically" goes *parabolic* by

300%—meaning drastically increases, all you earn is a 6% return. However, by owning shares, you would benefit from the 300% gain. This is the key difference between stocks and bonds.

Stocks = The consumer owns **shares** of a company and takes-part in the *profit and loss* (P&L) with medium to high risk for potential gains.

Bonds = The consumer is the lender and owns the **debt** of a company and/ or the government by loaning them money. Then earns an annual percentage yield (APY) with less risk, but does NOT take-part in the *profit and loss* (P&L).

Time & Money

Traditional investments typically require a long-term outlook to be appreciated and a nearsighted outlook will only lead to false expectations. Having long-term positions, in a *traditional investment*, is another key to becoming a financially fit because chances are you will need to make a combination of investments to be financially efficient. Investing has more to do with your perception of time than of money. WHEN you start investing, is just as important as HOW much. The bright side is traditional investments have a low barrier-to-entry, and a little goes a long way with *compound interest*.

- Compound interest is the interest you earn on interest returns from capital invested.

For instance, a person at age 25 contributing $200 per month into a retirement account with an average *annual percentage yield* rate (APY) of 8%, will earn more in interest with <u>less capital invested</u> than a person starting at age 35 contributing $500 per month—if the finish line was 65 years old. However, if you contribute $135 per month starting at age 20, you will surpass both individuals at ages 25 and 35 in interest gains. Investing at a young age and the power of compound interest can produce significant financial gains. Below are examples of the power of compounding interest.

Age: 20 to 65:
    Multiply: $135 a month x 45 years at 8% APY
    Score: = $580,053 total interest gains
    Total Capital Invested: $72,900

Age: 25 to 65:
    Multiply: $200 a month x 40 years at 8% APY
    Score: = $552,360 total interest gains
    Total Capital Invested: $96,000

Age: 35 to 65:
    Multiply: $500 a month x 30 years at 8% APY
    Score: = $528,806 total interest gains
    Total Capital Invested: $180,000

How To Make A Traditional Investment

Some companies offer employer-sponsored retirement plans as a 401(k) or employer-match 401(k), but as a financial athlete, it's all about putting in the extra work. Traditional investments such as stocks, bonds, Solo 401(k)s, 529 accounts, HSAs, traditional IRAs, and Roth IRAs allow individuals to save extra funds for retirement outside of their employer. In order to make traditional investments, one must first open a *brokerage account*.

- A brokerage account is an investment account held by a licensed investment firm. Brokerage accounts allows investors (meaning you) to purchase stock.

Brokerage accounts and investment firms are not uncommon and you've likely heard of some like *Vanguard*, *Fidelity*, *Charles Schwab*, *TD Ameritrade* and, of course, *Robinhood*. As always, consult with a certified financial planner (CFP) or certified financial advisor (CFA) to ensure that you are getting the most out of your money.

I'M PULLING UP ON MY CFP ASAP!

Now with the basics of traditional investments out of the way, here are a few things to note.

1. One attribute of traditional investments is its liquidity—meaning "easier" to withdraw cash when needed
2. There is a low barrier-to-entry for most traditional investments
3. There are usually no qualifications needed to participate
4. Require low upfront capital or collateral
5. Traditional investments are typically held long-term

Alternative Investments

Alternative investments, on the other hand, are a departure from traditional investments. There are many forms of alternative investments, which include *private equity, venture capital, hedge funds, private debt, commodities, real assets,* and intangible assets such as *intellectual property* (I.P.). The private sector of investing is not as heavily regulated by the *U.S. Securities and Exchange Commission* (SEC) as the public sector, so it's up to private investors to evaluate investments at their own risk. However, the SEC does require private equity firms to make distinctions between *accredited investors* and *non-accredited investors*—to set limits on who can invest.

MVP Terms Continued:

- The Securities & Exchange Commission (SEC) is a government agency responsible for regulating the stock market.

- Private Equity is capital invested into privately owned companies in exchange for equity. Private equity means the investment is not publicly traded in the stock market.

- Venture Capital is a form of private equity financing that venture capitalist or investors provide to start-ups or to small businesses that have growth-potential in exchange for equity in the company.

- A Hedge Fund pool investor funds to make high-risk investments for lucrative returns in exchange for fees and commissions.

- Commodity funds are investments in raw materials, natural resources, and infrastructure. Commodities can range from agriculture, such as coffee, wheat, and sugar; telecommunication, such as cell towers and satellites; precious metals, like aluminum and copper; and energy resources, such as oil and natural gas.

- Real Assets in alternative investments are tangible investments that hold value on their own. This includes real estate, art, collectibles, antique vehicles, memorabilia, and commodities.

- Intellectual Property (IP) is work, or invention, created by a person's or company's thoughts, ideas, and concepts. IP consists of copyright, trademarks, patents, trade secrets, publishing, branding, licensing, and NIL deals.

Alternative investments are more glamorous than traditional investments but here are a few important things to note.

1. Alternative investments are extremely illiquid—meaning once the investment is made its very difficult to get the money back.
2. The risk is very different from traditional investments
3. Typically investors must qualify to participate
4. Require more upfront capital or collateral
5. Can be held in either short-term or long-term positions

Some notable athletes with alternative investments include NBA Hall of Famer Shaquille O'Neal's with investments in sneakers and apparel, Krispy Kreme, fitness centers, and car washes; WNBA legend Angel McCoughtry, with investments in McCoughtry's Ice Cream, featured films and real estate; and NFL Super Bowl Champion Marshawn Lynch with his BEAST MODE multi-brand featuring a production company, blenders, and apparel.

S/O TO MARSHAWN!
HE PUT ON FOR
"THE TOWN"

Intellectual Property (IP)

When it comes to IP, which is mostly non-tangible assets, the two biggest names in the space is no other than Michael Jordan and Lebron James licensing their brands through Nike. Michael has been dominate with the Jordan brand shoes for nearly 30 years, but that's one of many ways to earn money through IP. Some could say Lebron dominates in media, film, and television—which is a space untapped by Jordan. The point being not all investments are tangible—meaning physical products. When Lebron and his team creates or *produces* a piece of media content like *The Shop, More Than An Athlete, Springhill, House Party,* or *Space Jam 2*, it generates income through sales, streams distribution deals, and *residuals*.

Similarly, athletes such as the Golden State Warriors' Stephen Curry have also gotten media and publishing deals to create and develop tv shows, film documentaries, and to write books. These are just a few ways athletes earn money through branding and licensing their name, image, and likeness —(NIL), which is also considered IP. Leveraging the rights to your name, image, and likeness can prove very lucrative as your popularity grows.

"I'm Not a Businessman I'm a Business, Man..."

Private Equity (PE)

Private Equity (PE) investing is investing in privately owned companies, established companies, sports teams, and commercial real estate, such as apartment buildings, hotels, shopping plazas, etc. Anyone who qualifies as an *accredited investor* and sometimes *non-accredited investor* can invest in private equity offerings. Qualified investors typically make the investment through a private equity firm that holds a separate fund for each investment. It's called private equity because these companies have yet to make an *initial* *public offering* (IPO) or do not plan on becoming publicly traded like other companies in the stock market. To invest in private equity, an individual(s) must qualify as an *accredited investor*. This means proof of earning $200k annually for two consecutive years or $300k with a spouse, possessing a net worth of at least $1 million, or successfully passing either the series 7, 82, or *65 exam.

(Story Time...)

In 2009, tennis legends Venus and Serena Williams became the first black women to own part of an NFL team—the Miami Dolphins. When the sisters became *limited partners* (LP) through their minority stake investment in the team, the Dolphins had an evaluation of $1.2 billion. Today, that value has risen to $4.6 billion. This is just one of the many alternative investments made by the sisters, who have diversified their portfolio with ventures in clothing, a sunscreen product line, and a superfood nutrition company.

#Private Equity

Before making any investment, traditional or alternative, there are a few things you must know. First, *never* invest in anything you are not willing to take the time to learn about! Be sure to seek council from experienced investors, CFAs, and industry experts to learn the pros and cons of the investment. Next, develop money management skills to better understand your finances in the event an investment goes against you. Last, know your risk tolerance and the risk of the investment. This is important because contrary to popular belief, most athletes lose their money due to bad investments decisions oppose to lavish spending and divorce.

Word Bro Cause Ain't No Way They Crashing Out Over Gucci...

CHAPTER   TWO

Estate Planning

Estate planning has many moving parts and can be difficult to navigate without the guidance of a licensed *Certified Financial Planner* (CFP), *Certified Financial Advisor* (CFA), and an *Estate Attorney*.

- Estate planning is the process by which individuals or family members arrange the transfer of their assets. Estate planning generally includes having a Will, Trust, Medical Power of Attorney, Living Will with Advance Medical Directives, Beneficiary Designation for Life Insurance and Assets.

What's important to understand is planning your estate can bring financial benefits while you are **ALIVE** and is applicable to any stage of life. Many families' estate plan to safeguard their wealth by keeping their assets inside of a trust, but it's also used to protect loved ones from lengthy and expensive probate judgements in the event of a family member's passing. Estate planning is often overlooked, but is one of the most proven ways to protect your wealth for the next generations to come.

"You make your own luck. You make it in training."
— Simone Biles

3

MORTGAGES

In basketball, you aim for the net; with mortgages, you aim for the equity. #facts

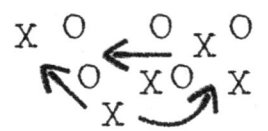

As intimidating as homeownership may seem, owning a home can be some of the most efficient debt an individual can have if purchased correctly. A mortgage is usually the largest debt an individual will gain throughout their lifetime, second to student loans and vehicle loans. Most people go from a car payment and a few thousand dollars in credit card debt to a mortgage. No doubt this can be a frightening endeavor, especially for new families, but before we get too far, let's discuss a few key terms you will need to understand in this chapter.

MVP Terms:

- A lender is a public, or private financial institution that loans or finances money to a borrower(s) under a contractual agreement to be paid back with fees and interest for a set term.

- A borrower is an individual or business that "borrows" money from a lender—public or private—under a contractual agreement to be paid back with fees and interest for a set term.

- A loan term is the agreed upon time the lender gives the borrower to repay the loan—usually expressed in months, quarters, or years.

CHAPTER THREE

- Principal balance is the amount owed to a debt obligation excluding interest, fees, and finance charges.

What Is A Mortgage?

A mortgage is the money a lender loans to a borrower or borrowers for the purchase of a home. To fully understand a mortgage, one must be aware of the cost and fees associated with it. A mortgage consist of four components, and when the homeowner makes a mortgage payment, the lender distributes the funds accordingly. To help memorize these four components, use the acronym "PITI."

P.I.T.I. PARTY!
PRINCIPAL, INTEREST, TAX, And INSURANCE x 2

PRINCIPAL is the part of the mortgage payment that goes directly toward the balance owed on the home loan.

Mortgage **INTEREST** is the annual percentage rate (APR) the lender charges the homeowner for the home loan.

Property **TAX** is the tax paid by the homeowner or entity that owns the property. This tax is based on the current value of the property and is assessed annually.

Homeowner's **INSURANCE**, or property insurance, protects the homeowner against damages and losses to the property and assets in the property. Depending on the policy, homeowner's insurance will also cover lawsuits from injured neighbors or visitors on the property, with exceptions.

Private mortgage **INSURANCE** (PMI) is a type of mortgage insurance required if a borrower does not put at least a 20% down payment. The purpose of PMI is to protect the lender if the borrower *defaults*—or fails to make their mortgage payments. PMI is usually 0.5% to 1.0% of the home loan—amortized at an annual percentage rate (APR) and typically falls off after 100 payments or roughly 9 years of homeownership. Most people view PMI as extra cost and a waste of money because it does not contribute to the principal balance, nor does it benefit the homeowner.

So, the homeowner pays for insurance protection of their home and insurance protection for the lender?

Unfortunately...

There are a few additional costs lenders may roll into the mortgage like *closing cost*—which are fees the lender charges to complete the home loan. Closing cost fees may include loan origination fees, attorney fees, title search fees, and more.

Boring, but important...

Types Of Mortgage Loans

There are several types of loans banks or lenders offer to qualified borrowers with the most popular being the FHA loan. Choosing the right type of loan can be critical to financial efficiency. There are loans specific to industries, income, and professions, and doing your homework can save thousands in homeownership.

An *FHA loan* is a government-backed mortgage insured by the Federal Housing Administration (FHA). The purpose of an FHA loan is to help low to middle class earners attain homeownership. FHA typically requires a lower minimum credit score and a lower down payment than conventional loans, however, these loans come with requirements the borrower must meet. *FHA loans can be used on single- and multi-family properties up to four units.

CHAPTER THREE

(Skip what doesn't apply...)

An *FHA 203(k)* loan is a government-backed mortgage that provides funds for rehabilitation and repairs to a damaged home to make a home FHA qualified.

A *professional mortgage loan* is a loan geared to towards borrowers practicing law or medicine. This loan gives borrowers in stable careers with high debt-to-income ratios, primarily caused by student loan debt, an opportunity to purchase a home. Banks realized career professionals in this subset may have large student loan debts with little savings established coming out of lengthy college programs. Do your research on which states and banks offer these types of loans. There is also a *Teacher Mortgage Program* most lenders offer for educators.

A *USDA loan* is a government-backed mortgage insured by the U.S. Department of Agriculture (USDA). The USDA loan caters to low-income residents of rural areas who cannot get approved for conventional loans. Some key benefits of this loan include zero down payment, no private mortgage insurance (PMI), competitive interest rates, lower closing cost, and relaxed credit requirements.

The *VA loan* is a government-backed mortgage insured through the U.S. Department of Veterans Affairs (VA). The VA loan is for service members and eligible members of the government. Some key benefits of this loan include zero down payment, no private mortgage insurance (PMI), competitive interest rates, lower closing cost, and relaxed credit requirements. Service members will need to visit the Veterans Affairs website for the full list of benefits and eligibility requirements. *VA loans can also be used for single- or multi-family properties up to four units.

A *conventional loan* is any conventional mortgage loan not insured or backed by the government. The minimum down payment for this loan is 3% but usually requires a higher down payment to be qualified.

WATER BREAK...

The House Buying Process:

1. Decide to buy a house → 2. Work with a licensed loan officer and real estate agent → 3. Obtain a Pre-Approval Letter → 4. Find a home in the budget of the Pre-Approval letter → 5. Home inspection and an appraisal → 6. Survive underwriting → 7. Close on property

There can be more or fewer steps to the home buying process, but the focus is on <u>steps 3 and 4</u>. These are the steps that can cause most borrowers to go from financially *efficient* to financially *inefficient* and exposes the critical difference between **QUALIFYING** and **AFFORDING**. What a borrower *"qualifies"* for may not be what they can *"afford"*. Let's start with qualifying.

"Shirts versus Skins"

Qualified Mortgage

The goal of this section is to help future homeowners understand the process in which lenders use to qualify borrowers. Qualifying means the lender is willing to loan the borrower the funds to purchase a home if they meet the requirements.

To qualify for a mortgage means you've applied for a home loan, and under minimal screening the lender sees you as a potential candidate to own a home. Next, the lender selects a loan officer in network, either internally or outsourced (third party), to gather financial documents from you—the borrower. The loan officer typically requests the following information:

- annual *gross* income (2 most recent tax returns)
- credit report
- pay stubs
- debt-to-income ratio (DTI) *gross*
- cash reserves (six months of bank statements)
- down payment amount

Do they need My Blood type too?

Loan officers use these financial documents to put together a certified pre-approval letter on behalf of the lender. The pre-approval letter is based on key information gathered from the borrowers financial documents. The loan officer uses this information to calculate the borrower's *maximum allowed mortgage payment*. The maximum allowable mortgage payment is what the lender believes to be the most the borrower can afford monthly. It's important to understand that the monthly mortgage payment will determine the *mortgage size*—meaning the price of the home.

The Maximum Allowed Mortgage Payment

When forming the pre-approval letter, the loan officer uses a *maximum allowable debt-to-income ratio* (DTI) that is set by the lender on a case-by-case basis. The maximum allowable debt-to-income ratio helps the lender determine the most the borrower's mortgage payment could be before adjustments. If it's an FHA loan, the maximum allowable DTI can be up to 50% to 56.9% of the borrowers monthly *gross* income—income before tax deductions.

Bro, This Like A Do it Yourself Kit!

Find The "Qualified" Monthly Mortgage:

For this example, we use the median annual *gross* income in the U.S. of $45,000 and the maximum allowable DTI of 50%.

Step 1: Monthly Gross Income

Calculate the monthly *gross* income by dividing the annual gross income by 12 months.

Divide: $45,000 annual gross income ÷ 12 months
Score: = $3,750 monthly gross income

Step 2: Maximum Mortgage DTI Before Adjustments

Next multiply the monthly *gross* income by the maximum allowable DTI of 50% or 0.50.

Multiply: $3,750 monthly gross income x 50% DTI
Score: = $1,875 maximum allowable mortgage

The maximum allowable mortgage payment for the borrower is $1,875, but there are still adjustments that need to be factored in.

Next, subtract the *minimum monthly debt payments* from the *maximum allowable mortgage* to find the *qualified monthly mortgage;* but first determine the minimum monthly <u>credit-reported</u> debt payments.

Step 3: Determine The Minimum Monthly Debt Payments

For this example, find the sum of a $100 minimum monthly credit card payment, a $150 minimum monthly student loan payment, and a $250 minimum monthly car payment.

Add: $100.00 credit card payment   +
Add: $150.00 student loan payment +
Add: $250.00 car payment   +

Score: = $500.00 minimum monthly payments

Note: Minimum monthly debt payments will vary for each individual.

If you recall, *debt payments* are only debts listed on the credit report.

Credit Reported Debt: (included but not limited to)

Housing	Car Payments	Second Mortgages
Credit Cards	Motorcycles	Construction Loans
Student Loans	Store Cards	Co-Signed Loans
Personal Loans	Financed Recreation Vehicles	Tax Installment Agreements
Lines Of Credits	Financed Furniture	Collections
Home Equity Lines Of Credits	Joint Loans	Government Mandated Payments

★ **Final Step:** The "Qualified" Monthly Mortgage

Calculate the adjusted "qualified" monthly mortgage by subtracting the minimum monthly debt payments from the maximum allowable mortgage.

Subtract: $1,875 max. mortgage — $500 min. debt payments

Final Score: = $1,375 "qualified" monthly mortgage

For this borrower, the most mortgage a lender is willing to approve is $1,375. If the borrower wants to be approved for more, they will need to add a co-borrower, earn more money, or reduce the minimum monthly debt payments.

Last, the pre-approval letter is sent to the borrower and real estate agent stating the prequalifying loan amount. Borrowers will have 60 to 90 days from the time of receiving the pre-approval letter, to find a home or they will need to reapply.

What's missing from this scenario is monthly **NET** income and **FIXED** and **VARIABLE** monthly _expense_ payments. Banks rarely include fixed and variable expenses when approving borrowers for home loans. Some instances when banks may include _expenses_ are home-related and income-related costs, such as *homeowners association dues* (HOA), child support, and alimony. When building your percentage-based budget, do not overlook fixed and variable expenses, as these payments often rival monthly debt payments.

Championship Mindset

We know from Chapter 1 that *gross* income is the employees' earnings before deductions are subtracted, but this is where the rubber meets the road. At this point, a decision must be made whether to let the bank determine what you can *"afford"* or decide for yourself. Remember, lenders view *gross* as real income; however, we know that *net* income is the real anchor for our budget. Just something to consider... Lock in!

THIS IS TOUGHER THAN I THOUGHT BRODIE!

"If you want to be good, you really don't have a lot of choices. Cause it takes what it takes. You have to do what you have to do to be successful. So you have to make the choices and decisions to have the discipline and the focus to the process to of what you need to do to accomplish your goals."

—Nick Saban

CHAPTER   THREE

(Story Time...)

During Hakeem Valles NFL rookie season as an Arizona Cardinal, he vowed to buy real estate in any city where he got drafted. When other players were financing million dollar houses, he used a $268,000 FHA home loan to buy a quadplex—a four unit multifamily house. Hakeem lived in one unit and rented the other 3 allowing him to live for free because he earned enough on the other 3 units to pay his mortgage. This enabled Hakeem to make other investments while having secure passive income to live on.

Dat man Smart...

After all, Warren Buffett still lives in a $32,000 home he purchased in 1958 with a current estimated value of $652,619. Even at the home's current evaluation, Warren Buffett's home still only represents .001% of his total net worth. What Warren Buffett understood is that if he purchased a house based on the percentage of his income, the house price would be in the billions, but instead, he opted for the house that suits his needs.

He Got That Dawg In 'Em

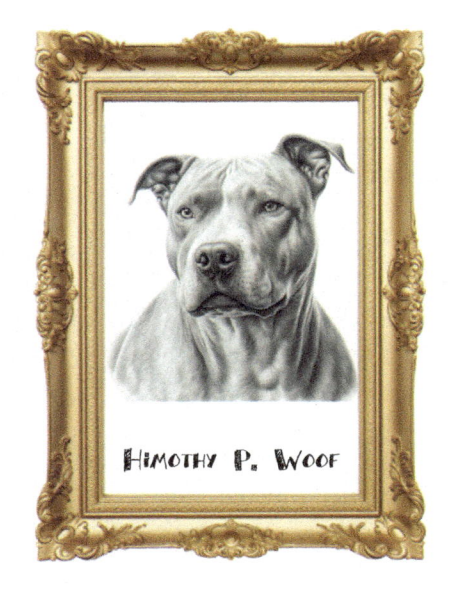

"Self Portrait"

Himothy P. Woof

HALF-TIME

Stretch... Hydrate... Communicate

"I couldn't beat people with my strength; I don't have a hard shot; I'm not the quickest skater in the league. My eyes and my mind have to do most of the work."
—Wayne Gretzky

Affordable Mortgage

Buying *"too much house"* can create a financially stressful environment for any homeowner—leading to anxiety over other outstanding debt and expense obligations. The term *"house poor"* refers to a homeowner spending so much on mortgage payments that there is little cash left for other financial obligations or personal saving goals. We also refer to this as being over-leveraged, if you recall from Chapter 1. Sometimes this happens because the homeowner did not consider all additional home costs associated with a mortgage, such as property taxes, home insurance, repairs, and maintenance. Other times, this happens because the homeowner purchases a home based on the lender qualifications. If one of the two spouses stops working for whatever reason, this could cost the homeowner(s) to become over-leveraged as well. Ultimately, buying too much house can limit your ability to save, invest, fully fund a retirement account, or pay off debt. This brings us to our next rule of thumb, *the 28/36 mortgage rule*.

The 28/36 Mortgage Rule

"Homeowners should spend no more than 28% of their monthly gross income on housing and housing-related expenses including HOA and Utilities—"

"—the total monthly debt payments should not exceed 36% of the homeowners monthly gross income including housing, credit-debt, vehicle, and student loans."

The purpose of the 28/36 rule is to keep homeowners in a more affordable mortgage without overextending their monthly income. If you recall, the maximum allowed DTI ratio for an FHA loan is 50% to 56.9%. According to this rule, it should be no more than 28%. We refer to the 28% DTI ratio as the *Affordable Mortgage DTI* because it's more align with what borrowers can afford. Keep in mind, this rule uses *gross*, **NOT** *net*, when calculating a mortgage.

Like the 50/30/20 rule, the 28/36 mortgage rule is applicable to roughly 95% of earners in the U.S.; however, our calculations are based on the median *gross* income of an individual earning $45,000 annually and an average mortgage term of 30 years. The 28/36 rule can be adjusted to fit most income levels but should be used with discernment for high *net* worth individuals. The overall point for this rule is to make a game plan when taking on debt.

28%
"Homeowners should spend no more than 28% of their monthly gross income on housing and housing-related expenses including HOA and Utilities—"

The 28% is the suggested percentage borrowers should allocate for housing and **ALL** housing-related expenses from their monthly *gross* income. This includes the mortgage (PITI)—principal, interest, taxes, homeowners' insurance, private mortgage insurance (PMI), homeowners' association dues (HOA), and utilities.

36%
"—the total monthly debt payments should not exceed 36% of the homeowners monthly gross income including housing, credit-debt, vehicle, and student loans."

The 36% portion suggests the sum of **ALL** household debt payments including mortgage, vehicle loans, student loans, and credit cards, should not exceed 36% of the monthly *gross* income. That's a 36% debt-to-income ratio across all debt payments.

As we apply the 28/36 mortgage rule, draw a comparison to the benchmark, The Rules of Thumb Stat-line, in chapter 1. While debts may vary by consumer, a visual representation of the *net* stat-line helps us deeply understand percentage-based budgets.

I'M READY O6!

CHAPTER   THREE

Find The "Affordable" Mortgage Using The 28/36 Rule:
For this example, use the median annual *gross* income in the US of $45,000 and the affordable DTI of 28%.

Step 1: Monthly Gross Income
Calculate the monthly *gross* income by dividing the median annual *gross* income by 12 months.

Divide: $45,000 annual gross income ÷ 12 months
Score: = $3,750 monthly gross income

Step 2: Affordable Monthly Mortgage
Next, multiply the monthly *gross* income by the affordable DTI ratio of 28% or 0.28, from the 28/36 mortgage rule.

Multiply: $3,750 monthly gross income x 28% DTI
Score: = $1,050 affordable monthly mortgage

From this example, we see the *"affordable" monthly mortgage* of $1,050 is less than the *"qualified" monthly mortgage* of $1,375, calculated on **page 49**. The difference between $1,375 and $1,050 is $325, which may seem insignificant but represents 11% of our percentage-based budget. In a game of inches, every percent matters!

The 36%…   TECHNICAL FOUL…

When we look at *the 28/36 mortgage rule*, some contradictions occur. There are a few rules discussed throughout this book that challenges the 36% portion of this rule. The 50% allocation for debt payments of **The 50/30/20 Budget Rule** does not coincide with the 36% total debt payment ratio of *the 28/36 mortgage rule*. The remaining rules in this book, such as **The 20/10 Credit-Debt Rule** and **The 20/4/10 Rule**, will easily put the debt payments above the 36% threshold. This may be achievable for some, but most will find a DTI of 36% across **ALL** debt payments unrealistic.

THE MATH AIN'T MATHING!

Although we've identified some discrepancies with the 36% portion of this rule, let's find the remaining percentage for debt allocation by subtracting 28% from the 36%. What remains is 8% for other debts such as, *student loan-, credit card-,* and *vehicle payments.*

★ **Final Step:** The Total Debt Allotment For The 28/36 Rule
Finally, multiply the monthly gross amount by 8%

Multiply: $3,750 monthly gross income x 8% or 0.08 DTI

Final Score: = $300 debt allotment

BRO HOW!?

The 36% portion of this rule limits borrowers to $1,350 in *total monthly debt payments* when earning a monthly *gross* salary of $3,750. That's $1,050 for **ALL** housing related cost and $300 for **ALL** other debts like *student loan-, credit card-,* and *vehicle payments,* etc. As previously mentioned, this may seem unrealistic but *the 28/36 mortgage rule* is just a guide and these totals can change drastically depending on if the borrower has little to no debt, a dual income household, or pays a significant down payment.

TEAM WORK MAKES THE DREAM WORK!

Find The "Affordable" Mortgage Debt-To-Net Income Ratio: Now the real question is, how much does the "affordable" mortgage consume of our **NET**—or take-home income? Use the "affordable" mortgage of $1,050 to find the debt-to-net income ratio (DTNI). But first, start by finding the monthly *net* income.

For simplicity, use the median annual *gross* income of a single individual earning $45,000 annually at a 22% federal tax rate. We did NOT include State tax, Medicare, Social Security, marital status, exemptions, and income tax brackets when calculating *net* income.

Step 1: Annual Federal Tax
Calculate the annual federal income tax deduction by multiplying the annual *gross* income by the federal tax rate of 22% or 0.22.

> **Multiply:** $45,000 annual gross income x 22% federal tax
> **Score:** = $9,900 annual federal tax

Step 2: Annual Net Income
Subtract the annual federal tax from the annual *gross* income. This will give the annual *net* income.

> **Subtract:** $45,000 annual gross income — $9,900 federal tax
> **Score:** = $35,100 annual net income

Step 3: Monthly Net Income
Calculate the monthly *net* income by dividing the annual *net* income by 12 months.

> **Divide:** $35,100 annual net income ÷ 12 months
> **Score:** = $2,925 monthly net income

★**Final Step: "Affordable" Mortgage Debt-To-Net Income (DTNI)**
Calculate the "affordable" mortgage debt-to-net-income ratio by dividing the "affordable" mortgage by the monthly *net* income. Then multiply by 100 to find the percentage.

> **Divide:** $1,050 "affordable" mortgage ÷ $2,925 monthly net income
> **Multiply:** = 0.35 x 100
> **Final Score:** = 35% DTNI

Based on this example, we see the *"affordable"* mortgage calculated using the monthly *gross* income, is actually 35% of our monthly *net* income. It's important to remember as we "stat-pad" our percentage-based budget *net* stat-line, to convert the debt calculated using monthly *gross* income to monthly *net* income. Now let's add our second *net* stat of 35% to our net stat-line!

LOADING...

Championship Finances
Monthly Net Stat-Line

Savings	Housing	Vehicle Payments	Credit- Debt	Student Loans	F/V Expenses
20%	35%				

100%
Monthly Net Income

Congratulations you made it to our second *net* stat! From this stat-line, we see that 20% of our *net* income goes towards **Savings** and 35% towards **Housing**—which equates to 55% *net* income allocated thus far. To achieve greater financially efficient, use the 28/36 mortgage rule with monthly *net* income instead.

Using The 28/36 Rule And Nothing But NET Income:

Building a percentage-based budget using *net* income can be a difficult feat, especially when trying to provide the best lifestyle for yourself and your family. However, if you want to truly stay on budget and remain financially efficient, take the ball into your own court and use nothing but net.

BRO LIKE YOU REALLY THE GOAT FOR THIS ONE!

Don't start glazing now…

CHAPTER THREE

"NOTHING BUT NET" MORTGAGE

★ **Find The "Nothing But NET" Mortgage**

Calculate the "affordable" mortgage by multiplying the monthly *net* income by *the 28/36 mortgage rule*.

Multiply: $2,925 monthly net income x 28% DTNI

Final Score: = $819 NOTHING BUT NET mortgage

Sheesh, can't buy nothing...

Using the 28/36 rule and the *net* income brings the "housing stat" down to 28%— demonstrating the difference between using *gross* income versus *net* income to structure debt. Hopefully, by now, you've gained a better understanding of the relationship between *gross* income and *net* income and the importance of creating a percentage-based budget. Use what you've learned so far to "stat pad" your own *net* stat-line.

> *"If you want to break through, your mind should be able to control your body. Your mind should be a part of your fitness."*
> — Eliud Kipchoge

"No Human Is Limited..."

The 28/36 Mortgage Rule comes in clutch to find an affordable mortgage payment, but to get a quick general guide for mortgage size, or home price, use the next rule; *the mortgage salary rule*.

The Mortgage Salary Rule

"Mortgage size should be no more than 2.5 to 3 times your annual gross salary."

When figuring out the mortgage amount or size, *The Mortgage Salary Rule* can be a useful tool. In finance, experts consider it safe to take on a mortgage that is 2.5 to 3 times the borrower's annual *gross* income, even with a small amount of debt. When borrowers opt for a mortgage that is 4 to 5 times their annual *gross* salary, it greatly increases the financial strain on their monthly *net* income—especially when there are additional debts, like credit cards, vehicle loans, and student loans.

Find The Mortgage Size:

Calculate the mortgage size using $45,000 to represent the annual *gross* income and *the mortgage size rule*.

Step 1: Mortgage Size x 2.5

Calculate the mortgage size by multiplying the annual *gross* income by 2.5**x**.

Multiply: $45,000 gross income x 2.5
Score: = $112,500 mortgage size

Step 2: Mortgage Size x 3

Calculate the mortgage size by multiplying the annual *gross* income by 3**x**.

Multiply: $45,000 gross income x 3
Score: = $135,000 mortgage size

To learn more about **The Mortgage Salary Rule**, amortization schedules, and how variations in mortgage terms and interest rates can affect your mortgage payment, turn to the next chapter.

Notes

_____
_____
_____
_____
_____
_____
_____
_____
_____
_____
_____
_____
_____

Chapter 3 Takeaways:
- Mortgage = "PITI" Principal, Interest, Tax, & Insurance
- Calculate what you can afford not what you qualify for
- Use Rules like the 28/36 Mortgage rule & the Mortgage Size rule to find an affordable mortgage
- Avoid buying "too much house" and becoming over-leveraged

4

MORTGAGE FUNDAMENTALS

Like a good point guard, a good mortgage rate can set the pace for your financial future.

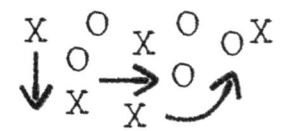

There are more ways to become financially efficient when purchasing a home other than the loan payment. The down payment and mortgage interest also plays a role in efficiency when taking on a mortgage. This chapter covers other financial tools, such as the amortization schedule—which will assist homeowners in making an informed decision on when to pay down, pay off, or invest. Last, we will look at the efficiencies in house hacking and the pros and cons of renting.

Let's Gooo!!

Down Payment

A down payment is a monetary payment to the principal balance of an asset at the time of purchase. A down payment can offer a slew of benefits to the homeowner. Paying a hefty down payment can significantly reduce the monthly mortgage payment and instantly establish equity in the home. Not to mention, if borrowers put at least 20% down, they may receive a better interest rate and will avoid paying private mortgage insurance (PMI). A hefty down payment also makes it less likely to go "upside-down" in the event there's a downturn in the housing market or catastrophic economic event. The term upside-down means you owe more on the home loan than the house is worth.

However, it's not wise to deplete your savings and emergency funds just to put 20% down on a home. If you have over 20% to put down, consider paying just enough to get rid of the PMI, as this can offer other opportunities to pay down *high-interest debts*, making your finances more efficient. Be sure to consult with a *Certified Financial Planner* (CFP) before making any drastic financial decisions to ensure you're getting the most out of your money. In most cases, you'll find that 20% is sufficient. The last thing a new homeowner wants to worry about is not having enough money in the event of an emergency or unexpected repair. Also, there are few homeowners willing to put old furniture in a new home, so be sure to consider the home and all its furnishings when purchasing.

I kept the Plastic on My Furniture...

The "NET" of it is you want to find a sweet spot for the amount you put down. Putting too much or too little down can make you less efficient as a borrower.

Mortgage Term

There are a few options for mortgage terms when purchasing a home. Borrowers can choose either a 15-year, 20-year, or 30-year mortgage term; however, due to inflation, the 40-year mortgage term has become the topic of discussion. If you recall, a mortgage term is the agreed time between the lender and the borrower to repay the home loan.

I Should've bought in the 5th Grade, 40 Years is Tough my Guy...

A 30-year mortgage term has become the industry standard because it offers a lower monthly payment than the 15-year term, which makes it easier for borrowers to qualify when applying for a home loan. Young borrowers typically start with a 30-year mortgage term, which is roughly 360 monthly payments, and once established in the workforce, can refinance to a 15-year term to save on interest and pay off their home loan faster.

The 15-year mortgage term is for borrowers who can afford to pay more monthly without financial stress. A 15-year mortgage term is roughly 180 monthly payments and borrowers who choose the 15-year term tend to be better established in the workforce and bring at least a 20% down payment. Otherwise, most borrowers will find it difficult to qualify for a 15-year mortgage term because the increased mortgage payment also increases the debt-to-income ratio, thus disqualifying the borrower from purchasing the home. No matter what term you choose, additional principal payments can be made to significantly lower the principal balance, reduce interest paid, and shorten the mortgage term.

Mortgage Interest

To remain financially efficient, borrowers must be aware of both the debt amount and the interest rate applied. Out of the hand full of interest rates to choose from, the two most popular options borrowers will consider are *fixed-rate mortgages* or *adjustable-rate mortgages*—(ARM). Since the 2008 mortgage collapse, fixed-rate mortgages have become a "crowd favorite" among borrowers who want a consistent interest rate for the duration of the home loan regardless of the housing market.

Unlike a fixed-rate mortgage, an adjustable-rate mortgage can "adjust" according to the market, but only after a predetermined fixed interest period, usually for the first 5- to 10 years, then the rate fluctuates either every 6 months or year. Some borrowers may opt for ARMs because they are easier to qualify for, since having a lower initial interest rate compared to fixed-rate mortgages.

Keeping a low interest rate on a mortgage does more for a borrower's financial efficiency than one may think. Remember, mortgage interest is the financing fee lenders charge borrowers' to loan money for a home. It can also significantly affect your DTI and the amount of cash flow left after making monthly debt- and expense payments. Mortgage interest rates can vary depending on your credit score, the housing market, Federal Reserve, economy, DTI, down payment, and mortgage term; however, in a stable market, your credit score and DTI will have the most impact.

Cumulative Interest

Interest on loans can be misleading because most borrowers view interest as a one-time fee, not a cumulative fee that recurs annually, hence the term APR—*annual percentage rate*. Not understanding how interest works can be detrimental to a borrower's financial efficiency long term. This applies not only to home loans but to all loans. For example, a loan with a 4% APR, means the borrower pays 4% interest on the balance of the loan **EVERY YEAR!!**

Year 1 annual interest 4% +
Year 2 annual interest 4% +
Year 3 annual interest 4% +
Year 4 annual interest 4% +
16% interest paid on principal

ALL THIS TIME I
BEEN GETTING GOT!

If You Don't Learn Anything Else, Know This!

From this brief example, we see the borrower has paid 16% in interest over the last 4 years. If we multiply the 4% annual interest rate over a 30-year term, the borrower will have paid 120% in cumulative interest. Annual interest and *amortization* is essentially why you pay nearly double for the home on a 30-year term.

Cumulative Interest + Amortization Nearly Doubles the Cost of a Home!

Amortization means to spread the cost of an asset long-term and for a mortgage, this is typically 30 years with interest. *The silver lining is the amount of interest paid is based on the principal balance, so the more you pay down the principal balance, the less interest you pay over time.*

Good, There Is Hope!

The Affects Of Interest

There are many benefits to keeping a low interest rate over the term of a loan. The average interest rate on a 30-year mortgage term as of this publication is 4.75%, with rates ranging from 2.75% to 7.25%. Buyers with excellent credit and shorter mortgage terms often have lower interest rates.

The example below shows the interest cost on a 30-year mortgage term for 3 individuals who has the same loan amount with different interest rates.

Note: Estimated mortgage payment calculated via www.calculator.net.

Ex. 1

Multiply: $300,000 mortgage loan x 4.00% interest rate
Score: = $215,609 interest paid over 30 years
Estimated Mortgage Payment: $1,432

Ex. 2

Multiply: $300,000 mortgage loan x 5.00% interest rate
Score: = $279,767 interest paid over 30 years
Estimated Mortgage Payment: $1,610

Ex. 3

Multiply: $300,000 mortgage loan x 6.50% interest rate
Score: = $347,514 interest paid over 30 years
Estimated Mortgage Payment: $1,897

If we compare the examples above, **Ex. 3**, paid $131,905 more for the same house, over the same period, than **Ex. 1**. From this scenario, **Ex. 1** is more efficient because of how much they saved in mortgage interest over the same 30-year term. This shows that every percentage point matter in financial efficiency.

Mortgage interest can drastically increase or decrease the monthly mortgage payment. A homeowner's interest rate can be the difference in the size and comfort of a home, the quality of life, access to better schools, and the neighborhood they live in. The reason is higher interest rates increase the mortgage payments, thus making it harder to qualify for the home.

Continuing with the same example above, **Ex. 1's** $300,000 home loan with a 4.0% interest rate, produced a mortgage payment of $1,432. If we compare the interest rate of 6.5% from **Ex. 3**, this increases the mortgage payment to $1,897. That's roughly a $465 monthly difference in mortgage payment for the same house and same mortgage term due to interest.

A $465 SAVINGS, NO BIG DEAL...RIGHT?

If **Ex. 1** invested the $465 monthly difference in an IRA at an 8.0% annual percentage yield (APY) rate of return (RoR) over a 30-year period, the contributions would have compounded to $491,790 in interest gains alone. That would make **Ex.1's** home close to being FREE! This shows the value of having good credit; why it's important to take advantage when interest rates are low; and the efficiencies of savings and investment planning.

OWE... BIG, BIG DEAL!

Amortization Schedule

An *amortization schedule* is one of the most underused financial tools available to borrowers. For most borrowers, unless they've purchased a home in the past, they've likely never seen or heard of an amortization schedule and seeing the imbalance of *principal* and *interest* for the first time may alarm you.

- An amortization schedule is a loan table that shows the annual periodic principal and interest payments made over the term or life of the loan.

In other words, an amortization schedule for a mortgage shows every principal and interest payment the homeowner will make for the entirety of the 30-year mortgage term.

IT'S THE MICHAEL JORDAN OF ALL FINANCIAL TOOLS...

30-Year Amortization Schedule

The goal of this section is to compare the 30-year and 15-year amortization schedules to detect efficiencies and inefficiencies in both. The 30-year amortization schedule will be borrower (A), and the 15-year schedule will be borrower (B). As you go through the following material, pay attention to the relationship between the *principal* and *interest*. Think of this schedule as the "scoreboard" for your mortgage payments.

The **Year 1** table shows the complete first year of interest and principal payments by month. This will help you visualize what's happening when you make monthly mortgage payments. An amortization schedule consists of a *beginning balance*, *ending balance*, *principal balance*, and *interest* owed; however, a complete mortgage payment consists of PITI. Just keep in mind an amortization schedule *ONLY* shows the "**P**"—principal and "**I**"—interest, of the mortgage payment but does **NOT** show the "**T**"—tax and "**I**"—for *private mortgage insurance* (PMI) and homeowner's insurance.

The example table below shows the parameters used to create a 30-year mortgage amortization schedule via www.calculator.net. Use **The Mortgage Salary Rule** of 3x the annual *gross* income of $45,000—to equate a $135,000 home price, (chapter 3, page 60); a mortgage interest rate of 4.75%; and an FHA loan down payment of 5.0%. This produces a mortgage payment of $1,016.51. Next, verify the *"affordable"* mortgage using **The 28/36 Mortgage Rule,** (chapter 3, page 53). Last, find the mortgage payment debt-to-*net* income ratio (DTNI) and review the 30-year amortization schedule.

Carolina Blue! For The GOAT, #23

Parameters For The 30-Year Amortization Schedule:

Mortgage Size (3x Annual Gross Salary)	$135,000.00
(5.0%) Down Payment	$6,750
Loan Term	30 Years
Loan Amount	$128,250
Mortgage Interest Rate	4.75%

CHAMPIONSHIP   FINANCES

Below are additional fields used to calculate the amortization schedule via www.calculator.net. Feel free to make adjustments to get familiar with amortization schedules.

Additional Fields via www.calculator.net:

Property Taxes 1.2%	$135.00
Private Mortgage Insurance 1%	$112.50
Homeowners Insurance	$100.00
Homeowners Association HOA	$0
Other Cost / Closing Cost	$0

Mortgage Payment, Gross & Net Income:

30 yr. Mortgage Payment	$1,016.51 ←
Annual Gross Income	$45,000.00
Monthly Gross Income	$3,750.00 ←
Monthly Net Income	$2,925.00 ←

Recall The 28/36 Rule from Chapter 3. This rule uses gross income.

Verify The 28/36 Mortgage Rule (30-Year Term):

Verify *the 28/36 mortgage rule* by dividing the mortgage by the monthly *gross* income. Then multiply by 100 to find the percentage.

Divide: $1,016.51 monthly mortgage ÷ $3,750 monthly gross income
                 Multiply: = 0.27 x 100
                     (**Score**: = 27% DTI)

PASS!!

The 30-year mortgage term debt-to-income ratio (DTI) falls within the 28% portion of this rule and gets the "*affordability*" pass when using the monthly *gross* income, but you know we use **NET** income!

CHAPTER FOUR

★ **Find The Mortgage Payment Debt-To-NET Income Ratio:**
Calculate the mortgage payment debt-to-net income ratio (DTNI) by dividing the mortgage payment by the monthly *net* income. Then multiply by 100 to find the percentage.

Divide: $1,016.51 monthly mortgage ÷ $2,925 monthly net income
Multiply: = 0.34 x 100
Final Score: = 34% DTNI

I MEAN, IT WAS CLOSE...

Year 1 By Month (30-Year Term) Amortization Schedule:

M	Beginning Balance	Interest	Principal	Ending Balance
JAN	$128,250.00	$534.38	$154.09	$128,095.90
FEB	$128,095.90	$533.73	$154.74	$127,941.16
MAR	$127,941.16	$533.09	$155.38	$127,785.77
APR	$127,785.77	$532.44	$156.03	$127,629.74
MAY	$127,629.74	$531.79	$156.68	$127,473.06
JUN	$127,473.06	$531.14	$157.33	$127,315.72
JUL	$127,315.72	$530.48	$157.99	$127,157.73
AUG	$127,157.73	$529.82	$158.65	$126,999.08
SEP	$126,999.08	$529.16	$159.31	$126,839.77
OCT	$126,839.77	$528.50	$159.97	$126,679.80
NOV	$126,679.80	$527.83	$160.64	$126,519.15
DEC	$126,519.15	$527.16	$161.31	$126,357.84

To see full 30 year monthly amortization schedule visit www.calculator.net.

In the first month, the **Year 1** table shows a significant disparity between interest and principal. This schedule can be alarming for first-time homebuyers unfamiliar with how *amortization* loans work. During most of the term, a greater portion of the monthly mortgage payment goes toward interest, PMI, and property tax. Therefore, many borrowers find that making additional principal payments is the most efficient way to manage mortgage interest. More on this in *Early Mortgage Pay Off* (see page 80).

CAN I HAVE SOME PRINCIPAL WITH THAT INTEREST?

Year 1-10 (30-Year) Amortization Schedule:

Y	Beginning Balance	Interest	Principal	Ending Balance
1	$128,250.00	$6,049.18	$1,978.94	$126,271.01
2	$126,271.01	$5,953.09	$2,075.03	$124,195.94
3	$124,195.94	$5,852.33	$2,175.79	$122,020.13
4	$122,020.13	$5,746.70	$2,281.42	$119,738.69
5	$119,738.69	$5,635.96	$2,392.16	$117,346.49
6	$117,346.49	$5,519.82	$2,508.30	$114,838.15
7	$114,838.15	$5,398.04	$2,630.08	$112,208.04
8	$112,208.04	$5,270.37	$2,757.75	$109,450.25
9	**$109,450.25**	**$5,136.49**	**$2,891.63**	**$106,558.57**
10	$106,558.57	$4,996.08	$3,032.04	$103,526.50

To build your amortization schedule, visit www.calculator.net.

By **Year 9**, or after roughly 100 payments, the homeowner satisfies *private mortgage insurance* (PMI) because they've added enough value into the home to reach the 20% equity requirement. *The homeowner may have to call the lender, at this point, to end the PMI payments.* If you recall, the bigger the down payment, the less you pay in PMI and if you pay a 20% down upfront, PMI is not required at all. Lenders do not display PMI on an amortization table, so keep this in mind.

100 PAYMENTS?! SMH

Year 11-20 (30-Year) Amortization Schedule:

Y	Beginning Balance	Interest	Principal	Ending Balance
11	$103,526.50	$4,848.88	$3,179.24	$100,347.23
12	$100,347.23	$4,694.56	$3,333.56	$97,013.62
13	$97,013.62	$4,532.69	$3,495.43	$93,518.17
14	$93,518.17	$4,363.00	$3,665.12	$89,853.02
15	$89,853.02	$4,185.07	$3,843.05	$86,009.93
16	**$86,009.93**	**$3,998.50**	**$4,029.62**	**$81,980.27**
17	$81,980.27	$3,802.86	$4,225.26	$77,754.98
18	$77,754.98	$3,597.73	$4,430.39	$73,324.56
19	$73,324.56	$3,382.64	$4,645.48	$68,679.06
20	$68,679.06	$3,157.11	$4,871.01	$63,808.02

To build your amortization schedule visit www.calculator.net.

From the **Year 11-20** table, we see that in **Year 16**, the principal balance begins to outweigh interest. Barring any refinances, now more of the mortgage payment goes towards the principal balance of the home loan than to interest, and making additional principal payments will only speed up this shift.

THAT'S CRAZY!

Year 21-30 (30-Year) Amortization Schedule:

Y	Beginning Balance	Interest	Principal	Ending Balance
21	$63,808.02	$2,920.64	$5,107.48	$58,700.51
22	$58,700.51	$2,672.68	$5,355.44	$53,345.03
23	$53,345.03	$2,412.70	$5,615.42	$47,729.56
24	$47,729.56	$2,140.05	$5,888.07	$41,841.47

CHAMPIONSHIP   FINANCES

25	$41,841.47	$1,854.21	$6,173.91	$35,667.53
26	$35,667.53	$1,554.46	$6,473.66	$29,193.85
27	$29,193.85	$1,240.20	$6,787.92	$22,405.89
28	$22,405.89	$910.67	$7,117.45	$15,288.39
29	$15,288.39	$565.11	$7,463.01	$7,825.35
30	$7,825.35	$202.81	$7,825.31	$0.00

To build your amortization schedule, visit www.calculator.net.

Looking at the complete 30-year amortization schedule, the total interest paid by borrower (A) was $112,594.58. Let's find the total cost of the home after 30 years or 360 mortgage payments.

Total Home Cost Of The 30-Year Mortgage:

Calculate the total home cost by adding the loan amount financed, down payment, and total interest paid over 30 years.

    Add: $128,250 loan amount financed + $6,750 down payment
            Score: = $135,000 home price

    Add: $135,000 home price + $112,594.58 total interest
        Final Score: = $247,594.58 total home cost

15-Year Amortization Schedule

Now let's look at the 15-year amortization schedule. A few things we can automatically assume is that the amount of interest paid over the life of the loan should be lower based on fewer years financed. Also, shorter terms typically have lower interest rates; however, the one tradeoff is a higher monthly mortgage payment. A higher mortgage payment increases the debt-to-income ratio, making it more difficult to qualify and even disqualifying some borrowers from receiving this loan term.

Listed below are the parameters used to create the 15-year amortization schedule via www.calculator.net. For comparison, we kept the parameters the same as the 30-year schedule.

Parameters For The 15-Year Amortization Schedule:

Mortgage Size	$135,000.00
(5%) Down Payment	$6,750
Loan Term	15 Years
Loan Amount	$128,250
Mortgage Interest Rate	4.75%

Additional Fields via www.calculator.net:

Property Taxes 1.2%	$135.00
Private Mortgage Insurance 1%	$112.50
Homeowners Insurance	$100.00
Homeowners Association HOA	$0
Other Cost / Closing Cost	$0

Mortgage Payment, Gross, & Net Income:

15 yr. Mortgage Payment	$1,345.07 ←
Annual Gross Income	$45,000.00
Monthly Gross Income	$3,750.00 ←
Monthly Net Income	$2,925.00 ←

Next let's verify 15-Year Mortgage Term using **The 28/36 Mortgage Rule**, the mortgage payment, and the monthly *gross* income listed above. Then calculate the monthly mortgage payment debt-to-net income ratio (DTNI).

KEEP THAT SAME ENERGY!

CHAMPIONSHIP　　　　　　　　　　　　　　　　　　FINANCES

Verify The 28/36 Mortgage Rule (15-Year Term):

Verify the 28/36 mortgage rule by dividing the mortgage by the monthly *gross* income. Then multiply by 100 to find the percentage.

Divide: $1,345.07 mortgage payment ÷ $3,750 monthly gross income
Multiply: = 0.35 x 100
Score: = 35% DTI

Fail!!

The 15-year mortgage's monthly payments was above the 28% threshold for this rule, making it less affordable.

★ Find The Mortgage Debt-To-NET Income Ratio:

Calculate the mortgage debt-to-net income ratio (DTNI) by dividing the monthly mortgage payment by the monthly *net* income. Then multiply by 100 to find the percentage.

Divide: $1,345.07 monthly mortgage ÷ $2,925 monthly net income
Multiply: = 0.45 x 100
Final Score: = 45% DTNI

Extra Fail!!
Let's Not talk About It...

Now let's look at the 15-year amortization schedule to see if we notice any major difference from the 30-year schedule.

(15-Year) Mortgage Amortization Payment Schedule:

Y	Beginning Balance	Interest	Principal	Ending Balance
1	$128,250.00	$5,962.19	$6,008.65	$122,241.35
2	$122,241.35	$5,670.48	$6,300.36	$115,940.99
3	$115,940.99	$5,364.60	$6,606.24	$109,334.76
4	$109,334.76	$5,043.89	$6,926.95	$102,407.81
5	$102,407.81	$4,707.59	$7,263.25	$95,144.58

CHAPTER　　　　　　　　　　　　　　　　　　　　FOUR

6	$95,144.58	$4,354.98	$7,615.86	$87,528.73
7	$87,528.73	$3,985.25	$7,985.59	$79,543.15
8	$79,543.15	$3,597.58	$8,373.26	$71,169.88
9	$71,169.88	$3,191.05	$8,779.79	$62,390.11
10	$62,390.11	$2,764.82	$9,206.02	$53,184.10
11	$53,184.10	$2,317.88	$9,652.96	$43,531.15
12	$43,531.15	$1,849.26	$10,121.58	$33,409.58
13	$33,409.58	$1,357.87	$10,612.97	$22,796.63
14	$22,796.63	$842.66	$11,128.18	$11,668.44
15	$11,668.44	$302.39	$11,668.45	$0.00

To build your 15 year amortization schedule, visit calculator.net.

Already, we can see the shift in interest to principal in **Year 1**. This shift did not occur until **Year 16** on the 30-year amortization schedule. The total amount of interest borrower (B) paid was $51,312.50. Find borrower (B)'s total home cost after 15 years.

Total Home Cost Of The 15-Year Mortgage:
Calculate the total home cost by adding the loan amount financed, down payment, and total interest paid over 15 years.

Add: $128,250 loan amount financed + $6,750 down payment
Score: = $135,000 home price

Add: $135,000 home price + $51,312.50 total interest
Final Score: = $186,312.50 total home cost

So, if we compare borrower (B) on a 15-year mortgage term paying $51,312.50 in interest payments to borrower (A) on a 30-year term paying $112,594.58, the difference is $61,282.08. Not to mention the benefits of owning a home 15 years sooner. In this scenario of strictly mortgage and interest, borrower (B) is more financially efficient.

Having A Game Plan Is the Key to Winning!

(Story Time...)

Daniel Norris, a MLB pitcher for the Detroit Tigers, is famously known for choosing to live the minimalist lifestyle. Daniel has received over $11 million in career contracts and in the offseason, Daniel lives in a $10,000 1978 Volkswagen Westfalia camper van named Shaggy. During the offseason, Daniel adventures cross-country trekking and surfing as a way of reflecting and refocusing for the next season. The lifestyle choice raised a few eyebrows with the general managers, coaching staff, and teammates, but Daniel found a lifestyle that works for him. Daniel didn't let his income dictate his lifestyle and found living frugal kept him grounded.

#VanLife

It's really you versus you out here...

HALF-TIME

Breathe... You Got This!

"Please don't allow my confidence to offend your insecurities. I truly believe in me 100%... If your dream isn't bigger than you, there's a problem with your dream."
— Deion "Prime Time" Sanders

"I ain't hard to find!"

Championship Mindset

Early Mortgage Payoff

Early mortgage payoff is a highly controversial topic in the world of personal finance. Past ideologies would suggest that there should be a sense of urgency and priority when paying off a mortgage. However, over the past 30 years, mortgage interest rates have dropped significantly from 19% to as low as 3.75%.

With low interest rates, some argue that finding other *investment vehicles* to park your money, such as an index funds or real estate, is worth carrying the mortgage full term. Another contributing factor is the change in mindset away from considering a house as an actual "ASSET." Many believe the power of investing is greater than the power of paying off low-interest debt like a mortgage.

Conversely, there are popular financial advocates with substantial research to support the claim that paying off all debt including the mortgage, while contributing to traditional investments is better overall for wealth building for the AVERAGE American. If you recall, traditional investments are stocks, bonds, cash, 401(k)s, 529 plan accounts, traditional IRAs, and Roth IRAs.

I SEE WHY WE WENT TO HALF-TIME...

Having virtually no debt offers a lot of lifelong tangible and intangible benefits, such as *equity*, *stability*, and *peace of mind*; however, no matter what side of the fence you sit on, there are a few things to consider when deciding to pay off, pay down, or invest.

I'M ALL EARS!

First, review the amortization schedule, because this will give a clear insight into what your mortgage interest is costing you each year. Next, conduct thorough research into what realistic investment opportunities are made available to you. Then, take inventory of how much cash you have on hand, including emergency savings. Last, sit down with a Certified Financial Planner (CFP) to compare your amortization debt and retirement savings versus traditional and alternative investments.

Homeowners may find it beneficial to do a little of both. Some homeowners opt for investing 15% to 20% of their income into traditional investments first, then making additional principal payments to their mortgage. Many homeowners make bi-weekly payments, which reduces the mortgage term on average by 5 to 7 years. This works because making bi-weekly payments equates to one additional payment each year. The impact additional payments has on the mortgage is highly underestimated. Paying a little extra takes years off the balance—resulting in better financial efficiency.

To Pay Off or Pay Down? That is the Question...

Mortgage vs High Interest Debt vs Investments
When deciding to invest, pay off a mortgage, or pay down debt, it's important to identify the difference between high-interest debt and low-interest debt. Many experts classify low-interest debt as debt with an interest rate below the stock markets average *rate-of-return* (RoR) which is roughly 8%. With that said, mortgage interest rates in good economic times are usually less than 8%—categorizing mortgages as low-interest debt. This is where the *"investing over paying of a mortgage"* debate stems from. The fact that you are earning 8.0% interest or more on an investment and only losing 4.0% interest or less paying on a mortgage, makes investing "seem"

like a more efficient use of discretionary income over paying down a mortgage. Essentially, the theory is you are earning more money on an investment than the mortgage is costing you, and based on the history of the market, consistent investments over a 30-year period can produce significant interest gains.

High-interest debt; however, is much different than low-interest debt. Paying off *high-interest* debt will certainly provide a better return on your money than almost any investment or mortgage pay off. In regards to interest rates, most consider mortgages, vehicle loans, and student loans to be *low-interest debts* and credit cards and personal loans to be *high-interest debts*. The average interest rate on consumer credit card debt in the US is 19.3%, and can top 29.9%. It's rare to find an investment that will pay you a return of 19.3% to 29.9%. So, when deciding whether to invest, pay off, or pay down—paying off high-interest debt seems to be the best choice.

Don't Take It Personal.
Either way, there is no one right answer in "personal" finances because let's face it, *"personal finance is personal,"* so you have a "personal" decision to make.

Mortgage Extension
There are many reasons why homeowners may decide to extend their mortgage term. On the surface, it may seem counterintuitive to reset your mortgage, but first, let's talk about how to extend a mortgage before we get into why.

Homeowners accomplish mortgage extensions via a loan restructuring called *mortgage refinancing*. We call this a "mortgage extension" because many homeowners don't realize they are resetting their 30-year mortgage with each refinance unless they specify. When a homeowner refinances a mortgage, the lender pays off the homeowner's original mortgage and underwrites a new one. Homeowners will need to provide a recent credit report, DTI, and sometimes an appraisal before final approval.

Why Extend?

There are a few reasons why homeowners may decide to refinance their mortgage. Either the homeowner wants to reduce their interest rate, reduce the mortgage payment, or withdraw equity. If the homeowner reduces their interest rate, this could mean saving hundreds on the mortgage payment. The combination of a lower interest rate and a new 30-year term can reduce the homeowner's mortgage payment and ultimately make the homeowner more financially efficient, but at the cost of resetting the mortgage term.

Cash Out Refinance

A cash-out refinance is when a borrower withdraws the equity from their home. *Home equity* is the difference between what the homeowner owes versus what the homeowner has paid toward the principal balance of their home loan, plus *appreciation*. Essentially, having a mortgage can be viewed as a "forced" savings account.

- Appreciation is the increase in the value of an asset over time.

Find The Home's Available Equity Balance:

Calculate the home's available equity by subtracting the balance owed on the home by the value of the home.

Subtract: $250,000 home value — $150,000 owed (balance)
Score: = $100,000 available equity

I Definitely Appreciate My Home!

A cash-out refinance is typically done when there is a significant amount of equity in the home. Lenders allow you to withdraw up to 80% to 90% of your home's equity for repairs, remodels, or debt consolidation. Homeowners will need to provide an updated appraisal, recent credit report, and DTI before final approval.

(Story Time...)

Since entering the league 21 plus years ago, Lebron James has been a very savvy investor, especially in residential and commercial real estate. Over the years, his properties appreciated by more than $50 million and today his real estate portfolio accounts for nearly $134 million of the billionaire's *net* worth. If he chooses, Lebron can draw from the equity in his properties for other investments.

Home Equity Line Of Credit (HELOC)

A home equity line of credit (HELOC) is a revolving loan that gives the homeowner access to the equity in their home. Lenders usually give HELOCs without having to restructure the current or original mortgage. This is possible because a home equity line of credit is a revolving loan separate from the original mortgage and uses the home's equity as collateral. However, if homeowners' default on their HELOC, they could risk losing their home. Lenders often refer to a HELOCs as a second mortgage.

That's the home court advantage!

House Hacking

House hacking is the use of a property you own or rent to generate income. House hackers achieve this by renting out additional spaces in their home, such as spare rooms, or getting permission from their landlord to sublease. Whether it's a single family, in-law suite, guest house, livable basement, or multifamily—maximizing additional space in the home to create income, can reduce monthly expenses, increase cash flow, and build home equity. The cash flow from rent can shave on average 10 years off the mortgage term if the rental income is applied to the principal balance of the mortgage. This makes house hacking one of the most financially efficient strategies in real estate.

The Efficiency Of Renting

That's Slick...

There's a common belief that by not becoming a homeowner and renting instead is waste of money. This is because the renter will never own the deed to the property. When renting long-term, you're missing out on home appreciation, equity, and protection against inflation. Rents can rise as much as 25% in a single year, but owning and having a fixed interest rate on a mortgage will protect you against rental hikes and inflation. However, let's look at the pros of renting.

When renting, you're paying for the freedom and flexibility to choose, swap up, trade down, or walk away at a rate a homeowner could never do. Renting also gives you access to a lifestyle you couldn't otherwise afford. It sounds counter efficient, but living in higher quality areas allows for more opportunities to network, because *"it's all about who you know."* If an area seems less safe, simply pack up and move. Renting lends the ability to try out different areas of a city, state, or country without commitment, which is difficult for a homeowner to do.

There are many added costs to homeownership, and not having the responsibility of property maintenance weighing on you may be what you need as you pursue a career or alternative investments. That's because renting allows more freedom to pursue investments or better job opportunities in other states. Not to mention, a smaller emergency fund is required, since there are minimal liabilities for repairs and maintenance. The average cost for renter's insurance is about $14 a month, which is a fraction of the cost for homeowner's insurance.

Another bonus is paying your rent on time can also help you build your credit. There are a few companies that will allow you to use your rent history to build credit. As always, do your due diligence to find the best company that works for you. Here are a few companies offering this service:

Good Lookin Out!

- Experian.com
- Rentreporters.com
- Rentalkharma.com
- Levelcredit.com
- Learn.Self.Inc

> "I am going to use all my tools, my God given ability, and make the best life I can with it.
> — Lebron James

Notes

Chapter 4 Takeaways:
- Cumulative interest is an annual fee
- Cumulative interest combined with amortization nearly doubles the cost of the home
- Amortization is the GOAT of Financial Tools
- A mortgage refinance often resets the loan term

5

VEHICLES

In Formula 1 it's all about precision and speed. Overspend and you might spin out of the financial race.

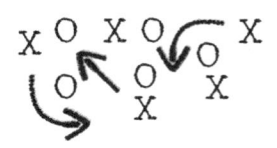

For many individuals, buying a vehicle can be one of the most expensive and emotional investments we make outside of purchasing a home. We use vehicles to make a statement about who we are or who we want to be and to express our personalities, community, lifestyle, religion, and socioeconomic status. We attach stickers of our political beliefs, the university from which we graduated, favorite sports team, and where our kids attend school. Seemingly, there's an endless amount of customizations to personalize our vehicles to our likeness. By human nature, we love to go fast and there is nothing like watching an engine and four wheels whip around a track at nearly 200 mph. However, as fun as it may be, vehicles still remain one of the most financially inefficient assets we can purchase.

Vehicle Use Cases

That F1 Though!

Convenience

The convenience of driving wherever and whenever you want can make life feel liberating. The ability to get back and forth to work more efficiently, among other duties, makes the convenience of owning a vehicle too valuable for most individuals to give up.

Employment

Using a vehicle to generate income has become increasingly popular over the last decade. There are many companies, such as *Uber*, *DoorDash*, *Lyft*, *Instacart*, *Amazon*, and *Turo*, that offer employment opportunities to drive and deliver on their platforms. There's no denying a depreciating asset can become an "asset," but is it enough to outpace the cost of vehicle ownership?

Status

It's no secret that some individuals purchase vehicles for socioeconomic status. Careers in real estate, finance, insurance, law, and entertainment are industries where a luxury vehicle is sometimes necessary to host clients. Those are usually niche markets where perception is king, and those individuals need their clients to know at a glance what level of success they've achieved, but is this the case for most?

(Story Time...)

In 2018, NFL quarterback Kirk Cousins signed a lucrative guaranteed contract with the Minnesota Vikings for $84 million. At the time, this made Kirk the highest paid quarterback in NFL history. Even with the new contract, Kirk still kept his beat up GMC passenger van he bought from his grandmother for $5,000 in 2014. Naturally teammates gave him a hard time, but Kirk doubled down by tweeting a picture of the van and stating, *"It's better to buy appreciating assets than depreciating assets."*

"You Like That..."

The Big 3 Of Vehicle Ownership

By many financial standards, a vehicle purchase can be one of the worst financial investments consumers will make throughout their lifetime despite its practicality. However, the idea is to reduce the amount of liability in vehicle ownership and not increase it by buying new. It's no easy feat to overcome the financial deficit of owning a vehicle, and here are the three reasons why.

1. Depreciation

As previously mentioned, most financial experts consider vehicles to be a depreciating asset.

- A depreciating asset is an asset that decreases in value over time.

This typically happens to vehicles because of the age, wear and tear, innovations in automotive technology, advancements in safety systems, modern styling, ecological and environmental changes and more. The pace of innovation, especially in todays times, can make a vehicle's value sink in a matter of months.

Like A Rock, IYKYK...

Depreciation of a new vehicle in the first year is around 20% in the U.S., with the first 10% decreasing in value as soon as you drive off the lot. In year 2, 3, and 4, the vehicle will continue to depreciate by a rate of 10% to 15% annually and tapers off to nearly 60% depreciation by year 5. Cars depreciate slower as they age and by purchasing a used vehicle, you let the vehicle go through the first few years of depreciation before purchasing. This allows buyers to purchase a used vehicle around its true value.

Depreciation Cliff Is Real!

No matter what a vehicle is used for, spending your income on a depreciating asset goes directly against financial efficiency.

However, through strategic purchasing, we can reduce the liability of vehicle ownership.

OK, I need Assets that Appreciate, Not Depreciate!

2. Interest

When a borrower finances a vehicle, they do so with fees and finance charges, mainly in interest. Depending on the buyer's credit score, down payment, and economic times, a vehicle's interest rate can range between 4% and 16%. Some may be lucky enough to get a 0% interest promotion at a dealership, while others may find themselves stuck in a predatory loan with interest rates as high as 29%. High interest are commonly associated with *"buy here, pay here"* dealerships. Buyers with little credit history and/or in financially distressed situations, are more susceptible to these types of *shark loans* and *predatory lending*.

Diabolical! Is That Legal?

Kind of, sort of…

Direct Financing vs Indirect Financing

By now, it seems the best way to buy a vehicle is with cash after the depreciation curve, but if financing is necessary, there are two options: *direct financing* and *indirect financing*. Direct financing is borrowing money directly from your local bank or credit union for the purchase of a vehicle. Prospective car buyers can apply at a branch or online, and upon approval, buyers can take the check to the dealership to find a vehicle within the approved loan amount. Car buyers who get direct financing often have more leverage to negotiate, get better interest rates, and have more freedom to explore different dealerships to find the right vehicle.

I don't Like this Game.

Indirect financing, on the other hand, is when prospective car buyers seek financing through the dealership. Opting for indirect financing can lead to the dealership's interest rate hikes, limit negotiating power, and discourage buyers from shopping around. This is because each dealership has to reverify, or "re-run" the buyer's credit—which can lower the buyer's credit score.

Beyond financing, there's still federal and state tax, warranties, and dealership fees that often get rolled into the loan—increasing the total cost of the auto loan. Additional costs not related to the vehicle can add thousands of extra cost to the loan balance and hundreds spent in interest payments annually. When this happens, the car buyer now owes more than the vehicle is worth and this is called being "upside down." Subsequently, paying interest on borrowed money for a depreciating asset is what makes vehicles historically a poor investment.

60% Depreciation... Interest What's Next?!

3. Maintenance, Warranties, & Insurance

The largest stream of income in the automotive industry is vehicle servicing. The servicing and maintenance of a vehicle, along with a few planned obsolescence, creates a very lucrative revenue stream for dealerships. If you understand the product and services model, it's not always about the initial sale, rather the residual dividend of replacing parts and repairing vehicles. According to AAA, the average annual cost of routine maintenance on a vehicle is about $900 a year, or $75 a month. That's the average cost of oil changes, air filters, brakes, rotators, fluid flushes, headlights, wiper blades, tire replacement, emissions testing, annual tag renewal, balance and rotation to name a few.

So, Depreciation, Interest, ~~Depression~~, & Maintenance

The cost of maintenance on vehicles with internal combustion engines (ICE) has made electric vehicles (EV), increasingly popular in recent years—beyond reducing the environmental impact.

Very few vehicle owners know that many manufacturers map out servicing for their vehicles to become obsolete after a certain period *"ALLEGEDLY"*; this is called *planned obsolescence*. This makes borrowers afraid to drive vehicles with expired warranties leaving no other choice than to roll the negative equity into a newer vehicle to repeat the cycle. Purchasing additional warranties is an option, but most opt to buy new to avoid more out-of-warranty repair cost. Coincidentally, a vehicle's warranty expires within 3 to 5 years, right on cue for the recommended time to upgrade your vehicle.

Auto Insurance — Got em In the Spin Cycle!

If you thought paying interest on a financed vehicle, enduring the depreciation curve, and maintaining it over many years was enough, now you must protect it. Auto insurance can be costly and is mandatory in most states. Having auto insurance legally protects the vehicle owner from damages, repairs, personal injuries, theft, accidental death, and even lawsuits in the event of an accident. The national average for auto insurance is $1,600 annually—or $133 a month. For young or reckless drivers, the amount can vary drastically. Also, vehicle owners with bad credit find they pay more for auto insurance than vehicle owners with good credit.

GAP Insurance — Filthy Work!

Guaranteed Asset Protection insurance (GAP) is additional vehicle coverage usually offered at the point of sale. This can be a onetime fee between $200 to $700, or added to the vehicle owner's standard insurance. GAP insurance covers the difference between what the vehicle owner owes versus the *actual cash value* (ACV) of the vehicle. In the event of an accident resulting in a *total loss,* or a vehicle deemed not repairable, your standard vehicle insurance pays the ACV of the vehicle. If the vehicle owner owes more than the vehicle is worth, GAP insurance covers the remaining balance.

The Big 3

The moral is it's hard to beat **THE BIG 3** of vehicle ownership: **Depreciation, Interest, & Maintenance**. *To pay interest, on borrowed money, for a depreciating asset, that you must maintain, is financially inefficient regardless of its necessity,* but for most of us, a vehicle is a necessity we can't afford to live without. The best we can do is limit the financial damage by making strategic purchases on vehicles.

That's A Wayne Gretzky Hat Trick on My Wallet!!

Too Much Vehicle

For all the reasons above, owning a vehicle is like kryptonite to financial efficiency. A vehicle too expensive can create inefficiencies in your finances, cripple your buying power, and make it difficult to get other loans, invest, or pay off debt. Too much vehicle can flip the dynamic of vehicle ownership to the vehicle owning you.

Efficiency In Vehicle Purchasing

There are guidelines for purchasing the right amount of vehicle that most buyers are not aware of—leading to dealerships being the buyer's voice of financial reason. (THAT PART!) *It's important to understand that dealerships sell to what the car buyer can afford in monthly payments and not the price of the vehicle; because dealers know that most consumers are* "PAYMENT BUYERS." This leaves buyers in overpriced vehicles with large monthly payments—which brings us to our first vehicle rule of thumb, *The "One Size Fits Most" Vehicle Rule.*

CHAPTER   FIVE

The "One Size Fits Most" Vehicle Rule

"The total vehicle price should range between 20% to 50% of the buyer's annual gross income, with a "one size fits most" cost of 36%."

This rule helps buyers quickly calculate the right price for an affordable vehicle and encourages buyers to analyze the *total vehicle price* instead of just the monthly payments. Purchasing a vehicle with an MSRP of $45,000 on a salary of $45,000 is not very financially efficient. *MSRP - *manufacturer's suggested retail price*. Keep in mind this rule is applicable to 95% of earners in the US; however, our calculations are based on the median annual *gross* income of $45,000. **(see income chart on page 26)**

TALK TO ME NICE...

Find The Maximum Vehicle Price:
Calculate the maximum vehicle price by multiplying the annual *gross* income by 50% DTI. Remember the range is 20% to 50%.

Multiply: $45,000 annual gross income x 50% DTI
Score: = $22,500 max. vehicle price

OK, NOT BAD!

According to this rule, $22,500 is the maximum vehicle price for an individual earning a $45,000 salary. Even at the top percentage of this rule, the vehicle price still seems reasonable. Before adding this rule to our percentage-based budget, we need to convert it from using *gross* income to *net* income.

Find The One Size Fits Most Vehicle Price:
Calculate the *one size fits most* vehicle price by multiplying the annual *gross* income by 36% debt-to-income DTI.

Multiply: $45,000 annual gross income x 36% DTI
Score: = $16,200 vehicle price

Now that we've found the total vehicle price at 36% using the "*one size fits most*" vehicle rule, next we calculate how much to put down, the length of the term, and the monthly vehicle payment debt-to-net income. This brings us to our next rule, *the 20/4/10 rule*.

The 20/4/10 Rule

(20) *"Put no less than a 20% down payment on the total vehicle cost."*

(4) *"The loan term should not exceed 4 years, or 48 months."*

(10) *"Vehicle payments and vehicle related expenses should be no more than 10% of the monthly ~~gross~~ [net] income."*

This rule sets guides and limits on how much to put down, the loan term of the vehicle, and the vehicle payment amount. Paying cash for a vehicle **AFTER** the depreciation curve is the most efficient way to purchase a vehicle, but it's not a reality for most. If you have the funds, paying cash for a vehicle can preserve cash flow, reduce financial liability, interest fees, warranties, and insurance.

20%
"Put no less than 20% down payment on the total vehicles cost."

The first part of this rule suggest to put at least 20% down when purchasing a new or used vehicle. A 20% down payment will reduce the amount owed and interest paid, making it more affordable when choosing a shorter loan term.

20%?
TAKE THE WHEEL.

It's giving broke...

I GOT TO MAKE IT TO THE LEAGUE BRO, THIS IS TOO MUCH!!

CHAPTER   FIVE

4 years
"The loan term should not exceed 4 years, or 48 months."

The second part of this rule suggests only financing a vehicle for a maximum of 4 years, or 48 months. A shorter loan term reduces the amount of interest borrower's pay over the life of the loan.

10%
"Vehicle payments and vehicle related expenses should be no more than 10% of the monthly ~~gross~~ [net] income."

Calculating the last part of this rule can be challenging because it requires including all vehicle expenses like car payment, loan interest, insurance, fuel, and maintenance, within 10% of the monthly ~~gross~~ [net] income. You know we use NOTHING BUT NET, so before adding this rule to our percentage-based budget, convert to *net* income.

ALL THAT IN THE 10%?! BALL CAP...

It's worth mentioning, that unless you make a significant down payment, 10% will be an ambitious goal for most. More often we find this rule keeps buyers in a range of 10% to 15% debt-to-net income, when paired with the *"one size fits most"* vehicle rule.

GAME RECOGNIZE GAME!

Remember, these rules are calculated using the U.S. median annual *gross* income of $45,000, and will need a great deal discernment for higher income earners. **(see income chart on page 26)**

Now let's work it out, but first, start by determining the monthly *net* income before calculating the total monthly vehicle cost at a 10% monthly debt-to-*net* income (DTNI).

97

Find The Total Monthly Vehicle Cost At 10% DTNI:

For simplicity, use the median annual *gross* income of a <u>single</u> individual earning $45,000 annually at a 22% federal tax rate. We did NOT include State tax, Medicare, Social Security, marital status, exemptions, and income tax brackets when calculating *net* income.

Step 1: Annual Federal Tax
Calculate the annual federal tax deduction by multiplying the annual *gross* income of $45,000 by the federal tax rate of 22% or 0.22.

Multiply: $45,000 annual gross income x 22% federal tax rate
Score: = $9,900 annual federal tax

Step 2: Annual Net Income
Subtract the annual federal tax from the annual *gross* income. This will give the annual *net* income.

Subtract: $45,000 annual gross income — $9,900 federal tax
Score: = $35,100 annual net income

Step 3: Monthly Net Income
Calculate the monthly *net* income by dividing the annual *net* income by 12 months.

Divide: $35,100 annual net income ÷ 12 months
Score: = $2,925 monthly net income

Next, calculate the total monthly vehicle cost at 10% debt-to-*net* income and at 15% debt-to-*net* income for comparison.

Let's Get It!
On to The Next One...

→

★ **Final Step:** Total Monthly Vehicle Cost At 10% DTNI
Calculate the total monthly vehicle cost at 10% debt-to-*net* income (DTNI) by multiplying the monthly *net* income by 10%.

> **Remember: The total vehicle cost consist of the car payment, loan interest, insurance, fuel, and maintenance.**

Multiply: $2,925 monthly net income x 10% DTNI
Final Score: = $292 total monthly vehicle

According to the 10% portion of **The 20/4/10 Rule**, a buyer with a monthly *net* income of $2,925 should spend no more than $292 in total monthly vehicle cost.

That's Clutch!

★ **Final Step Continued:** Total Monthly Vehicle Cost At 15% DTNI
Calculate the total monthly vehicle cost at 15% debt-to-*net* income (DTNI) by multiplying the monthly *net* income by 15%.

Multiply: $2,925 monthly net income x 15% DTNI
Final Score: = $439 total monthly vehicle

The 15% total monthly vehicle cost puts us out of the 10% range according to this rule, but is more in line with the average cost of a pre-owned vehicle in the US of $503 a month.

I don't Compete To Be Average!

PIT-STOP

Focus... Train... Execute...

"In racing there are always things you can learn every single day. There is always space for improvement, and I think that applies to everything in life."
— Lewis Hamilton

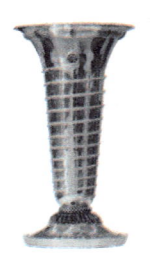

CHAPTER   FIVE

Championship Mindset

Practice Like You Play

True champions consider all possibilities, not only the ones set out in front of them. It's time to practice what we've learned and draw up a play with our two rules of thumb. In this section, we will use the previously calculated annual *net* income of $35,100, **The "One Size Fits Most" Vehicle Rule**, and **The 20/4/10 Rule** to calculate an *"affordable"* vehicle payment. Also, we will account for interest fees, sales tax, vehicle insurance, dealership fees, and other charges in hopes of maintaining a total monthly vehicle cost at 10% debt-to-[*net*] income. Last, we add our calculations to the *net* stat line.

Game Time!

Find: The One Size Fits Most Vehicle Rule – [Using Net Income]
To calculate the "one size fits most" rule—[using net income], multiply the annual *net* income by 36% to find the vehicles price.

> **Multiply:** $35,100 annual net income x 36% DTNI
> **Final Score:** = $12,636 vehicle price

$12.6K?? Bro, Yesterday's Price, Is Not Todays Price!

Find: The 20/4/10 Rule – [Using Net Income]
To determine the 20% down payment, we must consider additional expenses like sales tax, dealer fees, GAP, title, and registration. The vehicle's MSRP doesn't always reflect the total vehicle loan cost.

Step 1: Sales Tax
Calculate the sales tax by multiplying the vehicle loan amount by your states sales tax rate. For this example we use 8%.

> **Multiply:** $12,636 vehicle loan x 8.0% sales tax
> **Score:** = $1,010.88 sales tax

Step 2: Total Vehicle Cost

Vehicle Price	$12,636.00
Sales Tax (8%)	$1,010.88
Title & Registration	$600.00
GAP Insurance	$700.00

Add: $12,636.00 vehicle price +
Add: $1,010.88 sales tax +
Add: $600.00 Title +
Add: $700.00 GAP +
Score: = $14,946.88 total vehicle cost

Step 3: 20% Down Payment

Calculate the 20% down payment by multiplying the total vehicle loan amount by 20%.

Multiply: $14,946.88 total vehicle cost x 20% down payment
Score: = $2,989.37 down payment

The down payment for a vehicle is not included in the car loan so it must be subtracted from the total vehicle cost.

Step 4: Vehicle Amount Financed

Calculate vehicle amount financed by subtracting the down payment from the total vehicle loan amount.

Subtract: $14,946.88 total vehicle cost — $2,989.37 down payment
Score: = $11,957.51 vehicle amount financed

THAT'S TOUGH...!

Next, find the 4-year or 48 month term by first adding the monthly vehicle principal payment the average monthly interest payment.

Step 5: Monthly Vehicle Principal Payment

Loan Term	4 years or 48 Months

Calculate the monthly principal payment by dividing the vehicle loan amount financed by the selected term.

Divide: $11,957.51 total vehicle cost ÷ 48 month term
Score: = $249.11 monthly vehicle principal payment

For confirmation, apply the down payment into the auto loan calculator via www.calculator.net. This tool will show the complete *monthly* and *yearly* payment schedule for the vehicle loan on a detailed amortization table. **(see sample in step 6)**

Step 6: Find The Average Monthly Interest

Use the amortization table below to calculate the average monthly interest. The interest rate applied in our example is 6%.

Yearly Vehicle Loan Amortization Schedule:

Y	Beginning Balance	Interest	Principal	Ending Balance
1	$11,957.51	$643.27	$2,726.57	$9,230.92
2	$9,230.92	$475.11	$2,894.73	$6,336.16
3	$6,336.16	$296.56	$3,073.28	$3,262.86
4	$3,262.86	$107.02	$3,262.82	$0.00
	Total	$1,521.97	$11,957.51	

To calculate your vehicle amortization schedule visit www.calculator.net.

If we look at the interest column on the yearly amortization table, the total amount paid over the 4 years or 48 month term is $1,521.97. The interest will vary monthly so to make it applicable, divide the total by 48 months to find the monthly average.

T.R.O.F.E. NATION

Vehicle Interest Rate	6.0%
Total Vehicle Interest	$1,521.97

Calculate the average monthly interest paid by dividing the total vehicle loan interest by the 48 month term.

Divide: $1,521.97 total vehicle interest ÷ 48 months
Score: = $31.71 average monthly interest payment

Finding the monthly vehicle interest rate is difficult to calculate because the interest rate is amortized. The easiest way to achieve this is to use an online amortization calculator or use the *amortized interest trick* by doubling the interest rate. **6.0% x 2 = 12.0%**

Multiply: $11,957.51 total vehicle cost x 12.0% Interest
Divide: $1,434.90 total interest ÷ 48 months
Score: = $29.89 average monthly interest payment

Close Enough!!

Step 7: Vehicle Principal Payment + Interest

Calculate the total monthly vehicle payment by adding the monthly vehicle principal payment and the monthly interest payment.

Add: $249.11 monthly vehicle payment + $31.71 monthly interest payment
Score: = $280.82 total monthly vehicle payment

Step 8: Find The Vehicle Payment DTNI

Calculate the total monthly vehicle payment debt-to-net income by dividing the monthly vehicle payment by the monthly *net* income. Then multiply by 100 to find the percentage.

Divide: $280.82 total vehicle payment ÷ $2,925 monthly net income
Multiply: = 0.09 x 100
Score: = 9% DTNI

Pass!!
I'm Really Like That!

Not so fast **BIG BALLER!!** The last challenge is to see how we fare when we add the vehicle insurance and maintenance to the total monthly vehicle payment. (*Including other variables such as fuel cost is too broad for this calculation.*)

I WENT ELECTRIC HOMIE!

Step 9: Total Monthly Vehicle Cost

On average, Americans pay $1,600 per year or $133 per month for car insurance, as well as around $900 yearly or $75 monthly for routine maintenance.

Calculate the total monthly vehicle cost by adding the monthly vehicle payment, vehicle insurance, and vehicle maintenance.

> **Add:** $280.82 payment + $133 insurance + $75 maintenance
> **Score:** = $488.82 total monthly vehicle cost

Last step! Now that we have the total monthly vehicle cost, let's see if it holds true at a 10% debt-to-net income ratio.

AIN'T NO WAY BRO, I'M BOUT TO CRASH OUT!

★ **Final Step : Total Monthly Vehicle Cost DTNI**

Calculate the total monthly vehicle cost debt-to-net income ratio by dividing the total monthly vehicle cost by the monthly *net* income. Then multiply by 100 to find the percentage.

> **Divide:** $488.82 monthly payment ÷ $2,925 monthly net income
> **Multiply:** = 0.16 x 100
> **Final Score:** = 16% DTNI

FAIL!!
WITH A GRAIN OF SALT...

From this example, we get a debt-to-*net* income (DTNI) of 16% when following **The "One Size Fits Most" Vehicle Rule** and **The 20/4/10 Rule**—(using *net* income). Despite being 6% over the recommendation, this DTNI is still a good percentage. These rules are only guides and every consumer will have unique circumstances but the point is to have a game plan when purchasing a vehicle.

Now add the 16% total monthly vehicle cost to our percentage-based budget *net* stat-line.

LOADING...

Championship Finances
Monthly Net Stat-Line

Savings	Housing	Vehicle Payments	Credit-Debt	Student Loans	F/V Expenses
20%	35%	16%			

100%
Monthly Net Income

At this point, **Savings**, **Housing**, and **Vehicle Payments** account for 71% of our monthly *net* income. A few things to note, the vehicle payment calculations do **NOT** include additional *variable expenses* such as fuel, parking, tolls, valorem tax, or other deductions and fees that apply to your city and state. And If you live or work in the city—paying for daily street parking and tolls can add up. Also, living in rural areas can affect the price of fuel as well when commuting.

Other Ways To Reduce Vehicle Payments

The simplest way to lower your monthly vehicle payment is to extend the loan term. Some financial experts suggest a 36-month term for a used vehicle and a 60-month term for a new vehicle. Opting for a longer term will lower the overall monthly vehicle payments but will increase the interest paid over the life of the vehicle loan.

CHAPTER   FIVE

Next, buyers can increase the down payment on the vehicle loan and this will reduce the monthly payments. The 20% down payment is only a recommendation, so buyers can choose to put down what they can afford.

Also, comparing interest rates between banks can help reduce the monthly payments. Credit unions typically offer better rates than traditional banks. It's good practice to shop interest rates to find the best lender and rate before financing because vehicle interest can increase or decrease the monthly vehicle payments drastically.

Last, buyers can purchase a cheaper vehicle using the *one size fits most rule* at 25% annual debt-to-income. This will result in a more affordable vehicle and decrease the monthly vehicle cost.

So when can I get the Lambo...?

"When you have a goal that's important enough to you, nothing will stand in your way."
— Michael Phelps

Vehicle Leasing

Deciding to lease or buy a vehicle has been controversial in the world of personal finances for years. Whether you lease or buy, it still takes a great deal of preparation and understanding for the most efficient outcome. When leasing, a common criticism is that the lessee pays for the vehicle's initial 3 to 5 years of depreciation, with interest, without ever becoming the owner. The vehicle is owned by the financial institution. However, for some lessees, this lacks context. Now let's weigh the cons versus the pros.

Cons

One of the most important factors to consider when leasing is the mileage restrictions. Lessees have a certain amount they can drive each year, which is usually 10 to 12 thousand miles. Any miles driven over the mileage restriction by the end of the leasing term can result in fees. So, it's important to consider the distance between home, work, and entertainment before you lease. Another downside is at the lease-end, lessees have no guarantee of the same deal or interest rate and must pay a *disposition fee* to return the vehicle back into inventory. Not to mention, without *lease-end protection* or *excess wear and tear insurance*, the cost to return the vehicle can skyrocket. "All those fees...! Fuhgeddaboudit"

That's that New York...

When compared to leasing, buying can be a more financially efficient and preferable for individuals with longer commutes and need to travel without mileage constraints. Also, buying is a great option for those who want to lock-in an interest rate and plan to drive the vehicle for over 6 years. Ultimately, the decision to lease or buy will depend on your personal financial situation.

At "Lease" I Know what's Up...

CHAPTER FIVE

Pros

Leasing offers a lower monthly payment as financing a similarly priced vehicle. So, if you desire to drive a luxury vehicle or want "more vehicle", a good lease deal can cut the monthly payment by up to half—attracting *"payment buyers."* Also, since lessees have less liability for the vehicle, the financing institution and the dealership pay for most of the vehicle's maintenance and repairs. Let's look at the next rule to evaluate a "good" vehicle lease deal.

The 1% Vehicle Lease Rule

The monthly lease payment should equivalent to 1% of the vehicles price.

This means a $500 monthly lease payment on a vehicle priced at $50,000 is a GREAT deal—which is only 1% of the vehicle's price.

Calculate A Lease Offer Using The 1% Vehicle Lease Rule

Sample Lease Offer:

*MSRP (manufacturers suggested retail price)	$44,990
Lease Payment	$400 / monthly
Lease Term	36 months
Due At Signing First Months Payment, Security Deposit, Dealer Taxes, Fees, Registration, & Acquisition Fees	$3,000
*Money Factor	0.0032
*Residual Value	60%

*Note: Not all leases required to a pay a due at signing amount.

Step 1: "Actual" Due At Signing a.k.a. Down Payment
Find the "actual" down payment by subtracting the first months payment from the *due-at-signing* amount. The first months payment is included in the due at signing amount.

T.R.O.F.E.   NATION

> **Subtract:** $3,000 down payment − $400 1st month payment
> **Score:** = $2,600 actual down payment

Step 2: Monthly Down Payment Cost + Monthly Lease Payment

Calculate the monthly lease payments by dividing the "actual" down payment by the 36 month lease term.

> **Divide:** $2,600 down payment ÷ 36 month term
> **Score:** = $72.22 monthly down payment

Now roll the down payment into the lease payment by adding the monthly down payment to the monthly lease payment. This calculation assumes you put ~~ZERO~~ money down.

> **Add:** $72.22 down payment + $400 lease payment
> **Score:** = $472.22 monthly payment

Step 3: Sales Tax & Fees

Calculate the sales tax by multiplying the total monthly payment by the tax rate of 10.0%. **(tax rates may vary by state)**

> **Multiply:** $472.22 monthly payment x 10.0% sales tax
> **Score:** = $47.22 sales tax
>
> **Add :** $472.22 monthly payment + $47.22 sales tax
> **Score:** = $519.44 total monthly payments

★ Final Step: Monthly Lease-To-MSRP Ratio

Calculate the lease payment to *MSRP ratio by dividing the total monthly lease payments by the MSRP a.k.a. vehicle price. Then multiply by 100 to find the percentage.

> **Divide:** $519.44 total monthly payments / $44,990 vehicle price
> **Multiply** = 0.0115 x 100
> **Final Score:** = 1.15%

1.15%... YESSIR!
WHAT DOES THAT MEAN AGAIN?

Any lease offer requiring money *due at signing,* aka down payment, and has a percentage **LOWER** than 1.50% is a "good-ish" deal—at 1.25% an even better deal, but a **GREAT** deal at 1.00% or below.

Note, most dealerships do not require a potential lessee, with a decent credit score, to put money down. However, this changes the 1% rule slightly. So, a lease with *zero-down due at signing,* is now a "good-ish" deal at 1.00% and a **GREAT** deal at 0.75% or lower. Essentially, the lower the percent, the lower the risk for the lessee.

Some things to remember before putting money down on a lease. First, **YOU DON'T OWN THE VEHICLE!** Money down <u>decreases</u> liability for the financial institution, <u>increases</u> liability for the lessee, with the only benefit being a lower monthly lease payment. Second, in the event the vehicle becomes a **total loss*—meaning wrecked beyond repair, your down payment is forfeited.

Example: If a borrower **(A)** leases a vehicle with $3,000 *due at signing* and the next day it becomes a total loss, the $3,000 down payment is gone and does not transfer to a new lease. If a borrower **(B)** leases a vehicle with *zero-down due at signing* and the vehicle becomes a total loss, they can simply walk away. Keep in mind these are general principles of leasing and there may be more or less legalities, but the point is **YOU DON'T OWN THE VEHICLE!**

What's Affects Lease Payment
By now, you're probably wondering if a lease payment is really all just depreciation? Not necessarily, even though that's what we are often told. While it's true that the vehicle's value is decreasing, the monthly lease payment is determined by three factors: the *MSRP*, fees and taxes, the **residual value,* and the **money factor* (interest rate).

When shopping for a lease, be sure to ask about the money factor to determine the "finance cost" of the lease loan. Rarely do buyers ask about the money factor because many of us have never heard of it. When you lease, you are actually *financing the depreciation value of the vehicle* and anything with the word "finance," typically requires a credit check involving an interest rate. But because you are only liable for the depreciated value of the vehicle—not the vehicle itself, lenders re-package the term interest rate to "money factor"—defined as the financing fee for a monthly lease payment.

MONEY **F**ACTOR = **I**NTEREST **R**ATE!

Like an interest rate, the money factor will depend on your credit score and other economic factors at the time of purchase. The lower the *money factor*, the better payment for the lessee. In the leasing market, a money factor of 0.0035 is high, while 0.0025 is average. To better understand how money factor works, convert it to an interest or *annual percentage rate* (APR). Here's how:

Example:
Convert a money factor of 0.0032 into an *annual percentage rate* (APR) by multiplying the given money factor by 2,400.

Multiply: 0.0032 x 2,400
Score: = 7.7% APR

A more difficult way to calculate a money factor interest rate is to divide the lease charge by the capitalized cost plus the residual value —multiplied by the lease term. It looks something like this:

Money Factor = Lease Charge ÷ (Capitalized Cost + Residual Value) x Lease Term
$14,400   ÷   ($44,990   + $22,495)   x   36 months

MVP Terms:
- A lease charge is the total lease amount over the complete duration of the lease term—which in this example is 36 months.

Lease Charge: $400 monthly lease payment x 36 months = $14,400

- Capitalized cost is the vehicle price or MSRP of the vehicle.

   Capitalized Cost: $44,990 vehicle's MSRP

- Residual value is the estimated value of the vehicle at the end of a lease term—expressed as a dollar amount or percentage. For our example, use a residual value of 50%.

   Residual Value: $44,990 MSRP x 50% rv = $22,495 residual value

- A lease term is the duration of the vehicle lease, i.e. 36 months.

The Money Factor:

   Add: $14,400 ÷ ($44,990 + $22,495) x 36 months
   Divide: 14,400 ÷ (67,485) x 36 months
   Multiply: 0.21338 x 36 months
   Score: = 7.7% APR

Residual Value

Now, let's talk about *residual value*. The residual value is the estimated worth of the vehicle after the lease ends, sometimes expressed as a percentage. A higher residual value results in a lower monthly payment. For instance, if one vehicle retains 50% of its value and the other retains 60% over 36 months, which has the better residual value? The vehicle with 60% residual value because this means it depreciates less than the vehicle with 50% residual value. So, the vehicle with a 60% residual value vehicle will have a lower monthly payment. Last, the residual value determines the selling price of the vehicle from the lender at the lease-end.

   Multiply: $50,000 MSRP x 60% residual value
   Score: = $30,000 purchase price at lease-end

LET ME GUESS, IT'S THE "LEASE" YOU COULD DO!

6

CONSUMER DEBT

The best football players tackle their debt before they get sacked in the real world.

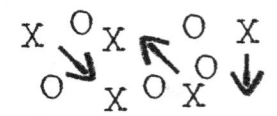

Understanding debt can be stressful, especially for young financial athletes looking to move up in the world. For most of us, we've heard the "debt" word thrown around our entire lives, with both good and bad connotations. As we've grown older, we still don't quite understand the true meaning of it. All we know is most of us will be in debt for the rest of our lives. This is partly because there are so many mixed signals around debt, such as:

"There's good debt and bad debt"
"It takes money to make money"
"Stay out of debt"
"Leverage debt to build wealth"
"Always use cash"
"Use other people's money—OPM"

I LIKE OTHER PEOPLES MONEY!

With so many contradictions around debt, no wonder most of us are stuck in a state of *analysis paralysis*—meaning too much information to make a decision. That's why it's important to be cognizant of who you gather financial information from, even if the one advising is an "expert." Certified Financial Advisors (CFA) and Certified Financial Planners (CFP) can only guide you. It's up to you to exercise the knowledge given and make wise decisions that work best for you. Let's set the foundation by reviewing the debt categories.

Secured Debt, Unsecured Debt, Revolving Credit-Debt, and Installment Debt

SECURED *debt* is money borrowed from a lender that requires collateral. Collateral is used for these types of loans as a backup in the event the borrower *defaults*—or fails to meet the payment obligations per the loan agreement. Lenders will use cash, vehicles, property, and other assets with monetary value as collateral. Lenders prefer secured debt over unsecured debt because it's less risky for them.

Note: Some publications may consider student loans as secured debt— using the students education as collateral.

UNSECURED *debt* is a debt which requires NO collateral from the borrower. Examples of unsecured debts are student loans, credit cards, lines of credit (LOC), and personal loans. Unsecured debt is riskier for lenders because there is no collateral required. To protect themselves from greater risk, the lender will rely on the borrower's credit history for final loan approval. Even though lenders prefer secured debt, unsecured debt is more common.

WHICH DEBT IS THE GOOD DEBT?

Some call it debt, some call it leverage…
You decide. It's personal bro…

REVOLVING *credit-debt* is when a borrower receives funds from a lender on a continuous basis with interest fees and monthly payments. What's unique about revolving credit is the borrower may continuously use the funds, pay it back, and borrow again as needed. When the funds are used, the revolving credit turns into revolving debt. Revolving credit-debt is often used interchangeably with *consumer credit-debt*. Revolving credit-debt can be classified as either secured or unsecured credit-debt but is typically unsecured. Credit cards and lines of credit (LOC) are examples of unsecured revolving credit-debt. Home equity lines of credit (HELOC) and secured credit cards are examples of secured revolving credit-debt.

Note: Lenders consider a home equity line of credit (HELOC), as a second mortgage. If the homeowner(s) default on the HELOC, they could risk losing the home.

LOANS = DEBT

INSTALLMENT *debt* is a type of debt typically used for a specific purchase. Installment loans can classify as secured or unsecured debt, but are more commonly secured. Examples of secured installment loans are auto loans and mortgages, but are also used to finance other items such as boats, motorcycles, or the latest iPhone through a cell phone carrier. Installment loans can require a short-term or long-term contractual commitment to repay the debt. Types of unsecured installment loans are personal loans, debt consolidation loans, and student loans.

Consumer Credit-Debt Spending

In this chapter, we focus strictly on unsecured consumer credit-debt spending, like unsecured revolving credit-debt, a.k.a credit cards, lines of credit, and unsecured personal loans. Revolving consumer credit-debt is the continuous use of money borrowed from a lender for the purchase of goods and services. Once the

CHAPTER SIX

funds are used, consumer credit becomes consumer debt, hence the term, *consumer credit-debt*.

Technically, all debt using credit is considered consumer debt including mortgages, vehicle loans, student loans, etc., but for context, we refer to *consumer credit-debt* as a result of spending consumer credit on goods and services.

So Basically Credit Cards...

What separates consumer credit-debt from nearly all other forms of debt is **HIGH-INTEREST**. As we've learned, vehicle loans, mortgages, and student loans are usually classified as low-interest debt and tend to have interest rates around or below 8%. Most consumer credit-debt has interest rates well above 8%, sometimes as high as 29%, with a national average being 19.3%. Therefore, many financial experts view *consumer credit-debt* as a financial ~~death wish~~, excuse me…, problem if held long-term.

Tell em How You really Feel!

However, consumer spending is the "heartbeat" of the economy and businesses know it. So much so that universities offer graduate level Marketing and Advertising (M&A) programs to learn human behavior and how to manipulate consumer spending habits—being that the majority of consumers are *emotional spenders*. The multi-billion dollar M&A industry sponsored by credit card companies was designed to amplify consumer spending—creating more *payment shoppers*. Ad campaigns enticing consumers to dine at certain restaurants, points for shopping at particular grocery stores—creates the latest **HYPE BEAST** trend to get customers to buy into a company's culture, beliefs, and rewards system.

Uh Oh, He on His Soap Box Bag...

The constant promotion of the *"buy now, pay later"* culture only further perpetuates consumerism and creates more *payment shoppers*. Consumerism has normalized the spending of future earnings on today's wants by convincing consumers to purchase nearly everything on credit. *Payment buying on credit is "bad" practice because it justifies purchasing items you couldn't afford or wouldn't have bought if you had to pay cash for it.*

However, the blame ultimately lies at the feet of the consumer to make smart decisions with their money. Unfortunately, consumer credit-debt usually comes with high-interest charges, which most can't afford, making credit-debt one of the least efficient types of debt to carry.

Before you borrow money, ask yourself, was I formally trained to manage money? For most of us, the answer is **NO!** By not taking the time to learn how to manage your own money, only increases the likelihood of mismanaging money borrowed from the bank or *other peoples money* (OPM). Which brings us to the next rule, *The 20/10 Credit-Debt Rule.*

I MISSED THAT TRAINING...

The 20/10 Credit-Debt Rule

"The total amount of consumer credit-debt <u>gained</u>, <u>held</u>, or <u>repaid</u> annually should not exceed 20% of their annual net or take-home income."
Exclude mortgage debt; [vehicle loan debt and student loan debt]

"—Consumers should spend no more than 10% of their monthly net or take-home income on consumer credit-debt <u>payments</u>."
Exclude mortgage payments; [vehicle payments and student loan payments]

YEAH, I GOT TO LOCK IN FOR THIS ONE...

CHAPTER SIX

> **FLAG ON THE PLAY**
>
> Special consideration for this rule is that most publications include vehicle loans and student loans in their equation, but exclude mortgage debt and mortgage payments. To make this rule applicable for most consumers, we've excluded mortgage-, vehicle-, and student loans since separate rules exist for them. From the research gathered when selecting this rule, we find there are many gray areas and this is only our perception of this rule.

20%

"The total amount of consumer credit-debt gained, held, or repaid annually should not exceed 20% of the annual net or take-home income."

Exclude mortgage debt; [vehicle loan debt and student loan debt]

This rule limits the total amount of consumer credit-debt an individual can GAIN, HOLD, or REPAY in a single year to 20% of the ANNUAL *net* income.

Note: "Repayments" are additional payments toward consumer credit-debt balances that's separate from the budget.

The reason for this rule is simple: to keep consumers *diversified* without them becoming over-leveraged. While it's crucial to quickly pay-off high-interest credit-debt, it's equally as important to prioritize *emergency savings*, *retirement savings*, and other traditional investments like *stocks*, *bonds*, IRAs, 401(k)s, *529 plan accounts*, etc.

THIS ONE'S TOUGH!

Find The Consumer ANNUAL Credit-Debt Limit:
For simplicity, use the median annual *gross* income of a single individual earning $45,000 annually at a 22% federal tax rate. We did NOT include State tax, Medicare, Social Security, marital status, exemptions, and income tax brackets when calculating *net* income.

Step 1: Annual Federal Tax
Calculate the annual federal income tax deduction by multiplying the annual *gross* income by the federal tax rate of 22% or 0.22.

> **Multiply:** $45,000 annual gross income x 22% federal tax rate
> **Score:** = $9,900 annual federal tax

Step 2: Annual Net Income
Subtract the annual federal tax from the annual gross income. This will give the annual *net* income.

> **Subtract:** $45,000 annual gross income − $9,900 federal tax
> **Score:** = $35,100 annual *net* income

★ **Final Step: 20% Annual Consumer Credit-Debt Limit DTNI**
Calculate the annual consumer credit-debt limit at 20% debt-to-net income by multiplying the annual *net* income by 20%.

> **Multiply:** $35,100 annual net income x 20% DTNI
> **Final Score:** = $7,020 consumer debt

Based on this example, this individual should not **GAIN** or **HOLD** more than $7,020 annually in consumer credit-debt. Any more than the 20% *annual consumer credit-debt limit* and this can lead to financial stress for the consumer.

Also, this individual should not **REPAY** more than $7,020 a year, or $585 a month, in <u>additional</u> payments toward consumer credit-debt balances according to this rule. Any more than the 20% *annual consumer credit-debt limit* and this can lead to neglecting emergency savings, retirement savings, and contributions to traditional investments. *Remember, repayments are additional payments toward consumer credit-debt balances that's separate from the budget.*

HALF-TIME

Breathe... Stretch... Hydrate...

"You have good days, you have bad days, but the main thing is to grow mentally." — "Hard work, dedication." — "All work is easy work."
— Floyd Mayweather Jr.

10%

"—Consumers should spend no more than 10% of their monthly net or take-home income on consumer credit-debt payments."

Exclude mortgage payments; [vehicle payments and student loan payments]

The second part of this rule suggests the sum of all consumer credit-debt **PAYMENTS**, such as *credit cards*, *lines of credit*, and *personal loan* payments, should be less than 10% of the **MONTHLY** net income—excluding *mortgage-*, *vehicle-*, and *student loan* payments!

Find The MONTHLY Consumer Credit-Debt Payments:
Step 1: Monthly Net Income

Calculate the monthly *net* income by dividing the annual *net* income by 12 months. Use the annual *net* income from previous section.

Divide: $35,100 annual net income ÷ 12 months
Score: = $2,925 monthly *net* income

★ **Final Step:** 10% Monthly Consumer Credit-Debt Payments DTNI

Calculate the monthly consumer credit-debt payments at 10% monthly debt-to-net income DTNI.

Multiply: $2,925 monthly *net* × 10% DTNI
Final Score: = $292 monthly credit-debt payments

Based on our example, this consumer should spend no more than $292 of their monthly *net* income on monthly consumer credit-debt payments. *To find your percentage, divide the total monthly consumer credit-debt payments by your monthly net income, then multiply by 100.*

Things To Consider

The 20/10 Credit-Debt Rule is a great guide to abide by when taking on consumer credit-debt, but it's important to know the challenges when applying it. First, joint credit cards or co-signed unsecured personal loans can make it difficult to maintain the annual credit-debt limit of 20%. Last, inconsistent pay from work or side hustles can make it difficult to calculate the annual and monthly *net* income needed to find the 10% monthly payments.

Now let's add the 10% monthly credit-debt payments to our percentage-based budget *net* stat-line.

Loading...

Championship Finances
Monthly Net Stat-Line

Savings	Housing	Vehicle Payments	Credit-Debt	Student Loans	F/V Expenses
20%	35%	16%	10%		

100% Monthly Net Income

With the addition of the consumer 10% monthly **Credit-Debt** percentage, it puts us at 81% debt-to-*net* income ratio. The silver lining of this stat-line is that we *"paid ourself first"* and got **Savings** out of the way. All that's left is to manage the rest of our debts and expenses. One more stat to go!

Bring us Home Student Loans....!

The "Benefit" Of Credit Cards
Credit Building

There are many benefits consumer credit cards offer, with the first being a low barrier to entry for establishing credit. For most of us starting off, we were told to get a store card, gas card, or student credit card as an initial way to establish credit. Some parents add their children to their credit cards to expedite the credit-building process in a method called *trade lining*. Either way, many credit lending companies understand the early frustrations of trying to establish credit and make concessions for individuals starting their credit-building journey.

Fraud Protection

When making purchases online, credit cards can be a shield between you and internet fraud. Exposing your personal banking information online, opens you up to more liability and using a credit card can reduce that risk. If your debit card gets hacked, the bank has less "skin in the game" in getting "YOUR" money back. Plus, bank fraud verification can take up to 60 days resolve and there is no guarantee you will ever recover 100% of your money.

On the other hand, if you use a credit card and it gets hacked, the liability falls on the credit card company. Now it's on the credit card company to get "THEIR" money back, as long as you report the fraudulent incident immediately.

THAT'S LOCKDOWN DEFENSE...

Rewards

Many savvy credit card users benefit from leveraging consumer credit to gain reward points. Credit card rewards have grown increasingly popular, as many use credit card rewards to offset the cost of travel. The more you spend, the more points you earn, and you can use those points to subsidize the cost of travel. Each credit card has unique benefits to match the individual traveler's needs. For example, one credit card will leverage points from grocery stores and dining out, and another card for flights and lodging. The key is to leverage points by spending money on everyday items you would normally purchase. However, the goal is to earn points and not pay interest. To avoid paying interest, zero out all credit balances before the due date. Reference *"How to Pay"* in the following section for further insight.

CHAPTER   SIX

Championship Mindset

Minimum Monthly Payments

Making the minimum monthly payments on a credit card is the least efficient way to repay high-interest debt. Every credit card billing statement will have a *minimum payment warning* followed by a repayment table. The statement below is for a consumer with a $10,000 debt balance—which is what the consumer owes—a 29% interest rate, and a minimum monthly payment of $200 a month.

Debt Balance	$10,000
Interest Rate	29%
Minimum Monthly Payments	$200

Minimum Payment Warning: If you make only the minimum payment each period, you will pay more in interest and it will take longer to pay off your balance.

If you make no additional charges using this card and each month you pay…	You will pay off the balance shown on this statement in about	And you end up paying an estimated total of…
Only the minimum payment	35 years	$51,967
$378	3 years	$13,614 (Savings= $38,353)

(Actual Credit Card Statement!)

Gave 'em a 3 Piece And a Biscuit...SMH

The table shows that if the consumer makes the minimum monthly payments of $200, it will take 35 years to repay the debt, but if they make monthly payments of $378, it will take 3 years to repay, barring any further charges. In this scenario, the 29% interest rate is a concern, but not the most important factor. If the consumer pays an extra $178 per month towards this credit card debt, it will reduce the payment schedule by 32 years, saving $38,353. The obvious comparison is if two individuals had the same debt balance and interest rate, who would be more financially efficient: consumer (A) paying $200 a month for 35 years or consumer (B) paying $378 a month for 3 years?

I know this one! It's (B)...

The Double-Edged Sword

You should always question taking on new credit debt, even if the funds are used for good reasons. New consumer credit-debt can present a new set of challenges but in today's time, it seems our needs and wants take precedence over what we can actually afford. This brings us to the double-edged sword of financial inefficiency, *high interest* and *high credit utilization*.

High-Interest Debt

Consumer credit cards are historically known for having high interest rates because of the upfront risk banks and credit card companies take when deciding to give consumers access to credit accounts. Even with the risk, lenders are not shy about putting money in the hands of consumers. In fact, the average credit card limit in the US is roughly $30,000. With high credit limits and interest, consumers can quickly find themselves in a *debt trap*. The truth is, you don't get a credit card because you want a good interest rate, and lenders are quick to give credit accounts because for lenders, the more you spend, the more they make. Credit card interest can be some of the most costly interest you can have, so it's important to keep your consumer credit-debt balances low.

The average interest rate for consumer credit cards in the U.S. is 19.3%, and the average consumer debt balance is $6,000. It's worth mentioning that most high interest consumer credit-debt comes from unforeseen circumstances. That's why it's imperative to build an emergency savings of at least 3 to 6 months, develop good money management skills, and commit to a budget.

How to Pay Credit Debt   **GOAT TALK!!**

The good news is that credit cards only charge interest when you use them and fail to pay the balance in full before the *payment due date*—which differs from the *statement date*. The *payment due date* is the deadline to make a minimum monthly payment. The minimum monthly payment is usually 1% of the balance including interest. If borrowers pay the debt balance in full during the grace period or by the payment due date, borrowers can avoid interest.

EURO STEP THE INTEREST...

The *statement closing date* refers to the last day of the billing cycle. On the statement closing date, lenders report the balance owed to the three major credit bureaus. This will affect your credit utilization and ultimately your credit score. The best outcome is to repay high-interest consumer credit debt as quickly as possible to remain financially efficient.

AHHH... THE OLD PICK & ROLL!

Billing Cycle: Jul. 1, 2050 - Jul. 31, 2050
A credit card billing cycle or billing period is the period between statement closing dates and is generally 28 to 31 days long.

Statement Closing Date: Jul. 31, 2050

Debt balances are reported to the Credit Bureau on the statement closing date. Pay debt balances down to at least 10% of the credit limit **BEFORE** the *statement closing date* to lower credit utilization and increase your credit score.

Pay Here to Increase Credit Score!

Grace Period: Jul. 31, 2050 - Aug. 19, 2050

Pay the full debt balance during the grace period to avoid interest charges. The grace period is between the *statement closing date* and the *payment due date*.

Pay Here to Avoid Interest!

Payment Due Date: Aug. 20, 2050

Payments made on or after the payment due date will accrue interest on the debt balance.

New Skill Unlocked!!

Delinquent Payment Reporting Date: Sept. 20, 2050

It's up to the lender to decide when to report delinquent or late payments which will **LOWER** your credit score. But this is typically done between 30 and 60 days past the *payment due date*. After this date the account will **DEFAULT!**

- Default is when the loan is delinquent for several months and the lender demands full payment before sending debt to collections.

Credit Utilization

Basically means it's Ova-Wit-Ta!

Credit scores are based on several factors from one of the most widely accepted credit reporting companies, FICO. FICO, which stands for *Fair Isaac Corporation*, developed methods of credit scoring for consumer credit based on five key factors obtained from the three bureaus: *Experian*, *Equifax*, and *Trans Union*.

CHAPTER SIX

The Five Credit Factors In Weighted Percentage:

- 35% payment history
- **30% amount owed (credit utilization)**
- 15% length of credit history
- 10% new credit or credit inquiries
- 10% credit mix (credit diversity)

FICO's second largest weighted metric for credit scoring is the *credit utilization ratio,* and it accounts for nearly one-third of the overall FICO credit score. The recommended range of a good credit utilization is 0% to 10% with the national U.S. average being around 25%. The more consumer credit-debt balances you have revolving, the lower your credit score will be. A high credit utilization affects the consumers' credit score and can cause future loan applications to get denied. So it's best to keep credit utilization low even if you use credit is for great investments.

The "NET" of it all is, paying a credit card company high interest on borrowed money while lowering your credit score due to increased credit utilization is what we call the *"double-edged sword."* This makes consumer credit debt the benchmark for financial inefficiency. (see page 162 for more on credit utilization)

That's A Double Tech...

"Fear comes in two packages—fear of failure and sometimes, the fear of success."
— Tom Kite

Notes

Chapter 6 Takeaways:
- The 4 types of debt: Secured, Unsecured, Revolving & Installment
- Credit justifies purchasing items you could not afford or wouldn't have bought if you had to pay cash for it
- Credit utilization and interest is the double-edged sword
- Review all Minimum Payment Warnings

You Matter... A lot!

7

Student loans

Train to control the debt like soccer players train to control the ball. Every successful player must learn to be a good debt defender.

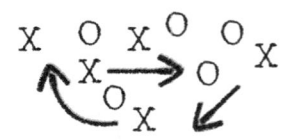

THIS WILL BE DRY... SO HYDRATE!

As demand for new technology and emerging markets grows combined with a significant increase in the cost of living, many students are feeling the pressure more than ever to stay competitive in the modern era. Society puts pressure on young adults to finish college from an early age—largely for job security and social validation. With higher-qualified candidates constantly entering the job market demanding better pay, the desire for a college degree, tech certifications, and higher education has become more sought after than ever.

However, it doesn't help when college tuition continues to increase every year at a rate exponentially faster than wages. This makes paying off those college debts challenging. Student loans can be essential for a young adult's financial growth, but on the other hand, student debt can make the road to financial freedom a rocky one. College debt can take a toll on a student's mental health and life goals, prompting a dire need for intervention in the collegiate system.

The Purpose Of Student Loans

Student loans fill the financial void that separates a student from their education. Lower- and middle-class families use it to bridge the gap between college savings and the remaining cost of education. With the rising cost of tuition, student loans are seen as saviors for a student's education and the key to a successful career. Students can use the funds toward their college tuition, living expenses, transportation, and other college expenses. However, college tuition rates continue to soar and more students require financial aid to build a better future for themselves.

Before applying for a student loan, it is crucial to understand the application process, qualification requirements, interest rates, and repayment terms. Let's explore the different student loans available in the U.S.

The Different Types Of Student Loans

There are two types of student loans—federal loans and private loans. The federal government grants federal student loans, while private organizations like banks and credit unions offer private loans. It's important to select the right loan that benefits you in order to remain financially efficient.

Federal Student Loans

As mentioned, federal student loans are loans granted by the federal government, and these loans have fixed interest rates and can offer flexible repayment plans under specific conditions. Students can apply for federal student loans by filling out a free application for Federal Student Aid, or FAFSA form. There are four types of federal student loans undergraduates can be eligible for: *direct subsidized*, *direct unsubsidized*, *direct loans plus*, and *direct consolidation loans*. In addition, under some circumstances, students can receive student loan forgiveness when they take out federal undergraduate and graduate loans.

(Skip what doesn't apply) I won't be Offended...

Direct Subsidized Loans

Direct subsidized loans, are federal loans for undergraduates where the student borrower is not required to pay interest while in school, deferment or during the grace period. Student borrowers are only required to pay interest if their class schedule drops below half-time enrollment, they leave college, or following the grace period, which is usually six months after graduation. The government calculates direct subsidized loans based on the students financial needs minus grants and scholarships the student may be receiving. These loans are financial aid to undergraduates who show they are in need and mainly available for low-income household families.

Undergraduate = Bachelors Degree Program

Direct Unsubsidized Loans

Direct unsubsidized loans are federal loans for undergraduates and graduates and its a non-need based, low-interest financial loan. Unlike the subsidized loans, unsubsidized loans generate interest the moment they are disbursed to the student. Like subsidized loans, student borrowers are required to pay interest if their class schedule drops below half-time enrollment, they leave college, or following the grace period after graduation.

Graduate = Masters Degree Program or Higher...

Direct subsidized and unsubsidized loans both have additional benefits, like flexible repayment options, low-interest rates, options to consolidate, deferment, and forbearance programs.

Federal Family Education Loan (FFEL)

A Federal Family Education Loan (FFEL) is a "hybrid" student loan. They work with private organizations to provide education loans backed by the government.

Direct PLUS Loans

A LITTLE OF BOTH, NICE!

Direct PLUS loans are available for graduates, professional students, and parents of undergraduates. It's called a Parent PLUS loan when borrowed in the parent's name and a Grad PLUS loan when borrowed in the graduate's or professional student's name.

Direct Consolidation Loans

These loans will enable student borrowers to combine many federal loans into a single loan entity. As a result, consolidation loans offer lower monthly payments and lower chances of default.

Private Student Loans

Private organizations such as banks and lenders—most commonly Discover, Citizens Bank, and Sallie Mae—offer private student loans. Applying for private student loans is straightforward but requires more than federal loans. Like federal loans, student borrowers must prove they are in college, but unlike federal student loans, credit score is more of a determining factor. Most students will have more of a challenge when applying for these loans because of unestablished credit. Interest rates on private student loans are flexible, and borrowers with excellent credit history can qualify for low interest rates. The rates can increase or decrease over time depending on the borrower's income level and market rates. Unlike federal student loans, you cannot get student loan forgiveness when taking out private loans. There are two eligibility categories you must keep in mind.

Undergraduate Loans
Undergraduate loans are for students who have not yet graduated. These loans are specific to undergraduates—meaning students working toward earning a bachelor's degree—and offer various repayment terms. It requires a co-signer who is an adult—usually a guardian—to be liable for the loan if the student borrower defaults. Private loans require a co-signer with a credit history since most undergraduate students are usually young adults and have had little time to build their creditworthiness.

Graduate Loans
Graduate loans are private student loans offered to graduates or professional students and they do not require a co-signer. Graduates or professional students are students who have earned a bachelor's degree and are pursuing higher level degrees. This type of loan option is best for law school, medical school, business school, etc. These loans can come with low interest rates and often have longer repayment terms.

The Student Loan Crisis

As of 2023, over 45 million Americans now have student loan debt worth nearly $1.7 trillion. This was a substantial increase since 1995 when it was around $187 billion. As government-owned student loan debt continues to soar, the topic has become increasingly heated. Many believe that the federal government should intervene and provide help to Americans struggling with student loan debt.

An Unwelcome Predicament
Nowadays, private and public colleges are listing tuition fees that are higher than the costs of attending college. As a result, the average student loan debt in the US is around $32,731. Despite repayment plans being structured as a 10-year plan, it takes an

average of 21 years for Americans to pay back their loans—which means late 30s and early 40s by the time the debt is repaid.

The average amount borrowed increases each year with inflation and so does the interest rates. However, the one thing that has not increased in over a decade is minimum wage. The U.S. has held minimum wage at $7.25 since July 2009. Combining all these factors, you can get a clear picture of why millions of Americans are struggling to pay off their student loan debt. It has become part of the culture, as more students take out student loans without understanding the long-term repercussions.

Championship Mindset

Borrowing With Salary In Mind

One of the biggest issues facing student borrowers is taking loans without knowing the earning potential of their degree post-graduation. It's financially inefficient to borrow $90,000 in student debt for a job with an annual salary of $45,000. Of course, each student should aspire to owe zero student loan debt and take advantage of scholarships, grants, 529 accounts, and state academic programs, etc.; however, that's not always possible. Students must weigh the cost of getting their desired degree versus their salary post-graduation. Like everything else, taking on too much student debt can put students in a *debt trap*.

- *A debt trap is when a borrower pays significantly more towards interest than to principal.*

There are three characteristics of a *debt trap* which are: *extended loan terms, 1% minimum monthly payments,* and *medium to high interest*. We call this the *"triangle offense"*. Loans categorized in this "offense" often result in minimum monthly payments consisting of 65% to 90% interest and if the borrower cannot afford to make additional principal payments, they could inadvertently be making interest-only payments! Meaning, the minimum monthly payments, which is usually 1% of the total loan balance, mainly satisfies the interest with little towards the principal balance.

Multiply: $100,000 student loan debt x 1%
Score: = $1,000 minimum monthly payment

Find The Interest-To-Payment Ratio:

For this example, calculate a monthly payment of $1,000, using an 9% annual percentage rate (APR), and a $100k student loan debt.

Multiply: $100,000 student loan debt x 9% interest APR
Score: = $9,000 annual interest

Divide: $9,000 annual interest payment ÷ 12 months
Score: = $750 monthly interest

Subtract: $1,000 min. monthly payment — $750 monthly interest
Score: = $250 monthly principal payment

★ Calculate the interest-to-payment ratio by dividing the monthly interest by the minimum monthly payment. Then multiply by 100 to get the percentage.

Divide: $750 interest payment ÷ $1,000 minimum monthly payment
Multiply: = 0.75 x 100
Final Score: = 75%

The amortized interest payment represents 75% of the monthly payment. This scenario would take the student borrower roughly 15 years to repay the debt—costing $85,000 in interest charges alone! And in 15 years, the total debt repaid will equate to $185,000.

That's BBQ Chicken...

Understanding the cost of obtaining a degree and the potential salary upon graduating is crucial to remaining financially efficient. This brings us to our next rule of thumb, *the student loan rule.*

The Student Loan Rule
10 | ≤ | 15

(10) *"The repayment of student loan debt should not exceed 10 years."*

(≤) *"The total student loan debt post-graduation should be no greater than the student's starting annual gross salary."*

(15) *"Student loan payments should not exceed 15% of the monthly net income."*

The purpose of *the student loan rule* is to educate students on how to borrow money for college while minimizing financial stress after graduation. This rule helps prevent student borrowers from over-leveraging their post-graduate future—which highlights the importance of establishing an *educational saving account* (ESA) early, such as a 529 plan account, UGMA, and UTMA. **(see page 147)**

AN UTMA? WHAT YOU CALL ME?

10 years
"The repayment of student loan debt should not exceed 10 years."

Students will often borrow so much in loans that it takes 10 years or more to repay. *Most students view debt as another obstacle that will work itself out post-graduation instead of moving through college with a plan to repay the money borrowed.* Regardless of the interest, aim to repay 10% of the principal balance every year after graduation to satisfy the loan in 10 years or less.

10 YEARS IS A MARATHON, BUT I CAN DO IT!

≤

"Total student loan debt post-graduation should be no greater than the student's starting annual gross salary."

This means if the student loan debt is less than or equal the student's starting annual *gross* salary, the repayment will be closer to a traditional student loan debt-to-income ratio (DTI) of 100%. While some may find this rule counter-efficient, student loan debt can often double the amount of the student's starting annual *gross* salary. Of course, it's better to budget these numbers using *net* income, but having student debt less than or near your starting annual *gross* salary will offer a better opportunity to repay the loan within 10 years without significant financial stress.

$45,000 student loan debt ≤ $45,000 starting annual *gross* salary

From this example, we see the student loan debt matches 100% of the students starting annual *gross* salary. Even though this rule allows student loan debt to match their starting annual gross salary, it reduces the financial efficiency of the student borrower and increases financial stress post-graduation. NOT RECOMMENDED!!

15%

"Student loan payments should not exceed 15% of the monthly net income."

Having student loan debt less than or near the student's starting annual *gross* salary is a quick way to gauge if you can repay your student loans within the 10 year timeframe. This rule helps keep student loan monthly payments below 15%; however, we do not recommend borrowing at the top of the suggested guide.

Are Rain checks an Option? Cause Bruuh!

CHAPTER SEVEN

Student Loan Amortization Schedule

Amortization schedules are useful for more than just mortgages. A student loan amortization table gives a 10-year outlook into what students can expect to pay monthly and annually, in principal and interest. It's important to use all financial tools available to make the best financial decision when borrowing debt.

The **Year 1** monthly amortization schedule shows the student borrower's monthly payments with $45,000 in student loan debt, 7% interest rate. This produces a minimum monthly payment of $522.49 over a 10 year repayment plan. The student is also has a starting annual *gross* salary of $45,000. With the annual *gross* salary and student loan debt both equaling $45,000, this should be the most college debt the student borrower takes on.

Below are the parameters used to calculate the **Year 1** monthly student loan amortization schedule via www.calculator.net.

Parameters For The Student Loan Amortization Schedule:

Student loan Amount	$45,000
Loan Term	10 years
Interest Rate	7%
Student Loan Payment	$522.49
Starting Annual Salary	$45,000

Student loan calculated via www.calculator.net.

Year 1 - Monthly Student Loan Amortization Schedule:

M	Beginning Balance	Interest	Principal	Ending Balance
JAN	$45,000.00	$262.50	$259.99	$44,740.01
FEB	$44,740.01	$260.98	$261.51	$44,478.51

CHAMPIONSHIP   FINANCES

MAR	$44,478.51	$259.46	$263.03	$44,215.48
APR	$44,215.48	$257.92	$264.57	$43,950.91
MAY	$43,950.91	$256.38	$266.11	$43,684.80
JUN	$43,684.80	$254.83	$267.66	$43,417.14
JUL	$43,417.14	$253.27	$269.22	$43,147.92
AUG	$43,147.92	$251.70	$270.79	$42,877.13
SEP	$42,877.13	$250.12	$272.37	$42,604.76
OCT	$42,604.76	$248.53	$273.96	$42,330.80
NOV	$42,330.80	$246.93	$275.56	$42,055.24
DEC	$42,055.24	$245.32	$277.17	$41,778.07

To see a full 10-year amortization schedule, visit www.calculator.net.

The **Year 1** monthly amortization schedule shows a fairly even balance between the interest and principal—at around 50/50 of the payment. Not bad, however; let's check the efficiency by calculating the student loan payment debt-to-net income ratio (DTNI), starting with determining monthly *net* income.

Find The Student Loan Payment Debt-To-Net Income:
For simplicity, use the median annual *gross* income of a single individual earning $45,000 annually at a 22% federal tax rate. We did NOT include State tax, Medicare, Social Security, marital status, exemptions, and income tax brackets when calculating *net* income.

Step 1: Annual Federal Tax
Calculate the annual federal income tax deduction by multiplying the annual *gross* income by the federal tax rate of 22%, or 0.22.

Multiply: $45,000 annual gross income x 22% federal tax rate
Score: = $9,900 annual federal tax

Step 2: Annual Net Income

Subtract the annual federal tax from the annual *gross* income. This will give the annual *net* income.

> **Subtract:** $45,000 annual gross income — $9,900 federal tax
> **Score:** = $35,100 annual *net* income

Step 3: Monthly Net Income

Calculate the monthly *net* income by dividing the annual *net* income by 12 months.

> **Divide:** $35,100 annual net income ÷ 12 months
> **Score:** = $2,925 monthly net income

★ Final Step: Student Loan Payment DTNI

Calculate student loan debt-to-net income ratio (DTNI) by dividing the student loan payment by the monthly *net* income. Then multiply by 100 to find the percentage. **(see chart on page 141)**

> **Divide:** $522.49 monthly payment ÷ $2,925 monthly net income
> **Multiply:** = 0.17 x 100
> **Final Score:** = 17% DTNI

From this example, we see that the $522.59 monthly student loan payment consumes 17% of the monthly *net* income. If you recall, 15% was our threshold according to **The Student Loan Rule**.

A lower student loan payment can be negotiated, but the student borrower would need to keep this pace in order to repay the student loan debt within 10 years. From this we learn it's wise to borrow significantly less than your starting salary in order to stay on track and reduce financial stress. Now let's add our final Championship Finances Monthly Net Stat-Line.

Let's Bring It Home!

CHAMPIONSHIP   FINANCES

Download Complete...

Championship Finances
Monthly Net Stat-Line

Savings	Housing	Vehicle Payments	Credit-Debt	Student Loans	F/V Expenses
20%	35%	16%	10%	17%	2%

100% Monthly Net Income

2%? Bruhhh...

The **Student Loan** payments brought us to the end of the regular season. The final 17% from student loans, puts us at 98% use of our monthly *net* income. Stick around ill the end for an *End of Season Review* to compare what we calculated versus the benchmark **Rules of Thumb Stat-Line** in chapter 1. **(see page 156)**

I don't know if I should Laugh or Cry?

Interest On Student Loans

Next, let's review the interest accrued over the 10-year amortization schedule using the same parameters as before.

Parameters Of The Student Loan Amortization Schedule:

Student loan Amount	$45,000
Loan Term	10 years
Interest Rate	7%
Student Loan Payment	$522.49
Starting Annual Salary	$45,000

Student loan calculated via calculator.net.

> *"Know the difference between enjoying your youth and destroying your future."*

10-Year Student Loan Amortization Schedule:

Y	Beginning Balance	Interest	Principal	Ending Balance
1	$45,000.00	$3,047.94	$3,221.94	$41,778.07
2	$41,778.07	$2,815.02	$3,454.86	$38,323.24
3	$38,323.24	$2,565.27	$3,704.61	$34,618.65
4	$34,618.65	$2,297.46	$3,972.42	$30,646.25
5	$30,646.25	$2,010.30	$4,259.58	$26,386.69
6	$26,386.69	$1,702.37	$4,567.51	$21,819.21
7	$21,819.21	$1,372.19	$4,897.69	$16,921.54
8	$16,921.54	$1,018.13	$5,251.75	$11,669.82
9	$11,669.82	$638.49	$5,631.39	$6,038.46
10	$6,038.46	$231.40	$6,038.48	$0.00

To see a full 10 year amortization schedule, visit www.calculator.net.

In the first year, this student paid $3,047.94 in interest and $17,698 over 10 years or 120 months. The total interest of $17,698, represents nearly 40% of the original $45,000 student loan.

Find The Total Student Loan Cost:

Calculate the total cost of student loan debt over a 10-year term by adding the student loan amount and the total interest.

Add: $45,000 student loan + $17,698.58 total interest

Final Score: = $62,698.58 total student loan cost

Student loan debt can cripple young adults looking to build a life post-graduation. Hopefully, student borrowers can better understand how to weigh the risk/ reward of borrowing money to finance their education. As always, the overall point is to have a game plan when taking on debt.

HALF-TIME

Hydrate... Focus... Relax

"Success is no accident. It takes hard work, perseverance, learning studying, sacrifice, and most of all love what you doing or learning to do."
— Edson "Pelé" Arantes do Nascimento

Educational Savings Accounts (ESA)

Educational Saving Accounts (ESA) are used for certain educational expenses for your children, other family members, and even yourself. The most popular ESAs include, 529 Plan, *Uniform Gift to Minors* (UGMA), and *Uniform Transfer to Minors* (UTMA)—which are all interest earning, growth accounts.

MVP TERMS:

- A 529 plan account allows tax-free savings for educational expenses of any student in your family or yourself. The longer the money is invested the more time it has to grow.

- UGMA/ UTMA are custodial accounts that are managed by a custodian, guardian, or parent to transfer assets to a minor; however, once the transfer or gift is made, it CANNOT be revoked.

Of course, there are many ways to save outside of these accounts and each plan will have its own unique advantages and disadvantages. Also, depending on the specific plan, an educational savings account can impact a student's eligibility for financial aid and annual tax benefits.

Maximize Your Student Loans

Sticking to a Major

When deciding to go to college, it's important to conduct proper research before selecting your degree. First, you need to know if you can see yourself committing to the desired career for at least a decade. Additionally, it's important to factor in the cost of the degree program and the earning potential before making a decision. If you enter college with these questions in mind and a game plan, this will prove beneficial for a couple of reasons. For starters, changing majors can cost a lot of time and money, especially if the degree is not in the same field as the original degree path. Last, sticking to one major will help you stay on track with graduation, limit further student loans, and get you into the work force sooner.

First Time Pass

Passing your classes is another crucial way of staying on budget with student loans but failing and having to retake classes means more cost. The average student finishes their undergraduate degree in 4.5 years, but failing classes can push the timeline to 5-6 years.

A+

Earning good grades can also be an efficient way to use student loans. Many students do not enter college with scholarships, but can get them along the way. Apply for as many scholarships and grants at the start and conclusion of each semester.

Intern

Internships, paid or unpaid, can offer several benefits for both the company and the student. Some companies will pay your tuition if the degree is beneficial for the company. This may require committing to the company for several years after graduation, but in most cases it's a win for both parties.

Alternative Education

That's The Win, Win!

Tech schools offer certifications for skilled labor such as electrical, welding, plumbing, emergency medicine, dental tech, carpentry, cosmetology, automotive, and more. Skilled labor is a faster approach to entering the job market because of a shorter degree and certification program. Skilled labor has the highest rate of entrepreneurs, and students who choose this path often out-earn their counterparts pursuing traditional degree programs. Most technical degrees involve manual labor; however, many students don't realize there are computer-based certifications also available.

Boot camps offer computer-based certifications in fields some companies do not require a degree for. This is prevalent in tech with careers like information technology (IT), cyber security, digital marketing, coding, and more. Amazon AWS is a mostly FREE tech learning platform has been a game changer for students with little money wanting to break into tech.

(Skip what doesn't apply) Seriously...

Creative Ways To Curve College Cost

There are many ways to curb the cost of student loan debt, some conventional and some non-conventional. Outside of tuition, the three major expenses most students face are housing, food, and transportation. Student loans can finance the cost of essential living items, including tuition, but if the aim is to cut costs, students must be creative. For example, working at a restaurant or grocery store can offer discounts on food. Living on campus can curb the cost of transportation, and having a roommate can help subsidize the cost of housing. Also, living at home while in college can save students thousands of dollars by the end of the degree program. If staying home is not an option, while living on campus, consider becoming a resident assistant (RA).

A resident assistant (RA) is usually a fellow student who monitors a designated dorm and enforces the rules and policies of the university. Some benefits of being a resident assistant during college are:

- free or discounted room and board;
- helps develop responsibility, management, and leadership skills

- great resume builder.

However, being an RA can be an enormous time commitment. To become an RA, you will need to apply through the university's federal work-study program, if applicable.

Federal Work-Study Program

The university's Federal Work-Study Program (FWS) could be another alternative. The federal work-study program is a part-time program with students working on average 10 hours per week, with a max of 20 hours. They gear this program toward students in financial need, but not all universities take part in the FWS program. Students will get paid directly as opposed to being deducted from college tuition. Examples of FWS jobs include but not limited to resident or community assistant, campus ambassador, teaching assistant, research assistant, library attendant, cafeteria worker, and tutor.

The university may also have an Institutional Work-Study Program (IWS). This program isn't "need" based, and students typically work in the department most associated with their degree. IWS jobs typically include research assistant and teaching assistant.

If campus work is not available, find jobs that offer tuition assistance or tuition reimbursement. Here are some jobs that have tuition programs:

- Publix (Publix Tuition Reimbursement)
- Amazon (Amazon Career Choice)
- UPS (Earn & Learn Program)
- Fedex (Fedex Tuition Reimbursement)
- Papa John (Dough & Degrees Program)

CHAPTER   SEVEN

- Starbucks (Starbucks College Achievement Plan)

I knew they had more than coffee...

There are also corporate partnerships between companies to offer tuition for their employees. Guild Education is the primary facilitator for tuition assistance to employers seeking to give their employees a chance at higher education.

Guild Education Partnerships:

Chipotle	Target	Walmart
Disney	Pepsico	Taco Bell
Lowes	Waste Management	Discover Financial

Freelance Work

A freelancer is a self-employed student or individual who offers services to clients on a project-to-project basis. This is an ideal way for students to make money for college expenses, as it allows them to easily fit it into their class schedule without having to commit to a full-time job.

Students can offer services such as cutting hair, cutting grass, car washing, cleaning, and laundry services to help with expenses, especially when some universities have 50,000 plus students on campus.

"You got to become a student of the game. You got to learn the game before you can go out there and play fast."

— Aaron Donald

(Story Time...)

Being a student athlete can have its perks from free housing, national recognition, and most importantly, taking advantage of a free education through athletic scholarships. One student athlete that maximized her time is none other than the Milwaukee native Dr. Valerie Daniels-Carter. Before the Phd, Valerie played collegiate basketball at Lincoln University in Missouri, where she would not only shine as an athlete but would earn a bachelor's degree in business administration. Her degree will prove handy as her career progresses. In 1978, the Milwaukee Does chose Valerie to play in the WNBA during the rise of women's professional sports. However, after a few practices, she had to decline the opportunity and became a banker to provide for her family after her father's passing—as the women's professional league was in its infancy and had limited sustainability during this time.

While in banking, Dr. Valerie Daniels-Carter earned a master's degree in business management from Cardinal Stritch University and started V&J Holdings, INC. with her brother John Daniels Jr. —an attorney graduate from Harvard Law. Valerie and John would franchise and develop over 100 quick-service restaurants including 36 Burger King, 68 Pizza Hut, 5 Haagen-Dazs and enter a joint venture with Shaquille O'Neal to run 11 Auntie Anne's Pretzel stores. This would make her one of the largest female owned franchise organizations in the country, while remaining an avid sports fan. Her business prowess would catch the eye of the Green Bay Packers front office and in 2011 she became the first African-American woman elected on the board of the Packers organization.

In 2014, Dr. Valerie Daniels-Carter joined an investment group called *Partners For Community Impact* and together would make

CHAPTER SEVEN

a minority stake investment in the Milwaukee Bucks NBA team—becoming the first African-American female to own a stake in an NBA franchise.

In 2021, the Bucks would win their second NBA Championship title since 1974. Dr. Valerie Daniels-Carter career accolades are just a small part of all the philanthropic work she has done worldwide, particularly for women across Africa.

Made Her-Story!

Student Loan Repayment Terms

For student loan repayment plans, there are a variety of options. Student borrowers can go with the standard repayment plan, which includes a fixed interest rate—keeping the same monthly payments for the loan term.

A graduated repayment plan is a plan where the loan payments start low and gradually increase every two years or so. A graduated repayment plan is common for careers that require one to two years' experience before a large salary increase.

An extended repayment plan allows students to have more time to pay off their loans, with a 20-year to 25-year term. However, despite having low monthly payments, this repayment plan can lead to accruing interest for a longer period.

Last, there are income-based repayment plans where repayment terms depend on one's income. Nevertheless, students still end up accruing more interest the longer the term.

Student Loan Pay Off Strategies

Refinancing is an excellent method to consider when trying to accelerate paying off student loan debt. Essentially, you're taking out a loan with an interest rate lower than your student loan debt and replacing it with a new one—usually from a private lender. Refinancing student loans is an option for both private and federal loans. However, by refinancing federal student loans, you waive the right to student loan cancellations and forgiveness programs.

The purpose of refinancing is to lower the interest rate and reduce the monthly payments, saving thousands over the lifetime of the loan. Students can find a multitude of private lenders, including banks and credit unions that offer student loan refinancing.

Students with federal loans can also consolidate their student loans rather than refinancing. This involves combining multiple federal loans into a single loan with one simple monthly payment.

The Debt Avalanche Method
Another great way to pay off student loan debt is by following the debt avalanche method. In this method, place all your student loans in order with the highest interest rate on top. Then, you look to pay the loans with the highest interest rates first, so they don't accrue higher debts later. Once the higher-interest loans are eliminated, pay off the next highest. Wash, rinse, and repeat until all debt is gone.

The Debt Snowball Method
The debt snowball method is a self-paced debt reduction strategy that suggests paying off lower debt balances first and saving the high debt balances last regardless of interest rate. Student borrowers can achieve this by paying down small debt balances aggressively while making minimum payments on the larger balances. Once a student pays off one debt, they use the additional funds to pay the next debt—until all debt is eliminated.

CHAPTER   SEVEN

HYDRATE!!

Additional Principal Payments

If possible, try to make additional principal payments each month. Making additional payments towards the principal balance will shorten the loan term, as this helps to prevent interest from accruing. Think of it like this: Making two student loan payments per month can help you pay it off twice as fast.

Using 529 College Savings Plan

In recent years, the government has allowed students to pay their student debt by using a 529 savings plan. Initially offered as a way for parents to save college funds for their child, in 2019, the government declared student loans as a qualified expense when using a 529 savings plan. The government allows a student to use up to $10,000 to repay their student loans.

Student Loan Consultant

A student loan consultant can assist in guiding students to pay off their student debt quickly and efficiently. They are certified industry experts who help students follow the right strategies to pursue their debt freedom goals.

> *"I trained 4 years to run 9 seconds. There are people who do not see results in two months, give up and quit."*
> — Usain Bolt

END OF SEASON REVIEW

The number's are in and it seems that we've manage to stay within 100% of our monthly *net* income using the rules of thumb. By creating a percentage-based budget, hopefully this book illustrates a few key take-ways. First, the importance of each percentage-point relating to monthly *net* income and how quickly it can be consumed with debt. Next, the difference between using *gross* income to structure debt versus *net* income. And last, how we can allocate our *net* income by creating a percentage-based budget.

HIMOTHY!

Rules Of Thumb
Monthly Income Stat-Line

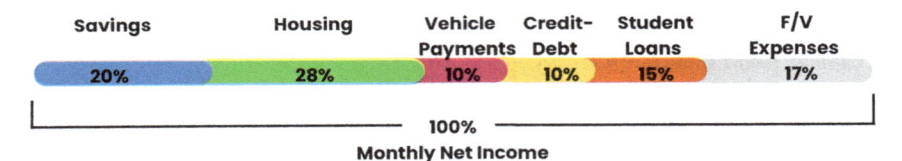

Savings	Housing	Vehicle Payments	Credit-Debt	Student Loans	F/V Expenses
20%	28%	10%	10%	15%	17%

100% Monthly Net Income

Champion Finances
Monthly Net Stat-Line

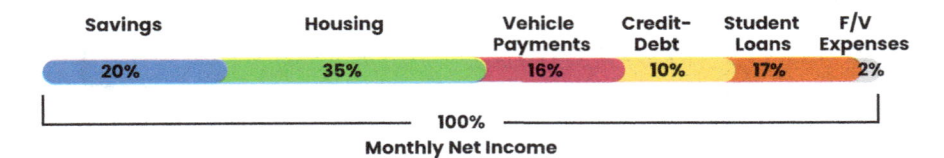

Savings	Housing	Vehicle Payments	Credit-Debt	Student Loans	F/V Expenses
20%	35%	16%	10%	17%	2%

100% Monthly Net Income

Now let's go stat-for-stat and compare our original **Rules of Thumb Stat-Line** from chapter 1 to our **Championship Finances Monthly Net Stat-Line**. The Championship Finances Monthly Net-Stat Line was created by analyzing the rules of thumb in each chapter and using the debt-to-*net* income from each rule to get a percentage. If you look at both stat-lines, it's apparent that structuring debt based on *gross* income doesn't give us a clear financial game plan. The remaining 2% for fixed and variable expenses on the Champion Finances Net Stat-Line is significantly less than the 17% on the Rules of Thumb Stat-Line. This is because the debt-to-*net* income percentage increased the monthly debt payments when compared to using *gross* income. Additionally, we pushed the limits of the "rules" to assess the worst-case scenario. Now the only option for acquiring more funds is to withdraw from savings—which we want to avoid. When creating your a percentage-based budget, focus on reducing costs in each debt category, beginning with the back-end budget, which includes structured debt items.

Each individual will have different debt obligations and unique circumstances that will affect their percentage-based budget. So, it's important to build a strong financial team of people you trust, as well as consulting experts like CFPs and CFAs. Be sure to set short-term and long-term savings and investment goals, then get the people in your "huddle" on board with your game plan. Remember, the goal is to lower debt, save money, increase investments, and most importantly, have FUN while doing so! Thank you for giving your all and I'll see you next season!

LEAVE IT ALL OUT ON THE FIELD!

"Wins and loses come a dime a dozen. But effort? Nobody can judge that, because effort is between you and you."
— Ray Lewis

"Crown"

BONUS CHAPTER

Put in that work this off-season.
And remember the long way is the short cut...

8

CREDIT

With great [credit] comes great responsibility!

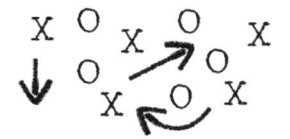

A credit score is simply a tool for financial institutions to measure the probability that a borrower will repay their debts. We shouldn't look at credit as an obstacle but as an opportunity. With a good credit score, borrowers can benefit from applying for loans with ease while enjoying the cost-savings from lower interest rates compared to *subprime borrowers*—a person considered high risk to lenders. Use these concepts in this chapter to build and understand credit to be more financially efficient when taking on debt.

Everyone must learn about credit and understand how to build good creditworthiness if they want to remain financially efficient. Having a healthy credit score could save you money by receiving loans with lower interest rates when purchasing assets such as houses or vehicles. Also, good credit helps when applying for different loans, and allows you to rent with fewer deposit fees. In addition, your credit score can play a role when getting consumer goods and services like new cell phones, car insurance, and utilities.

The good news is that you don't need to be a finance guru to understand credit.

This guide will teach you all about credit—how to build a good credit score and how credit scores work. Once you've understood the fundamentals of good and bad credit, you will be on course to save money in the years to come while having better leverage on investments involving credit.

The Three Bureaus

There are three credit bureaus that determine a consumer's creditworthiness—which is an individual's likelihood of repaying their debt or defaulting on their debt obligations. To default means failing to repay a loan, which everyone should avoid. The big three credit bureaus in the U.S. are Equifax, Experian, and TransUnion. This trinity of bureaus compiles credit reports and scores by collecting and analyzing information received from financial institutions to create a consumer's creditworthiness.

Each credit bureau has its own internal process to gather information about consumers, compile credit reports, and calculate the appropriate credit scores based on their internal parameters. Your standard credit report contains personal information like your name, address, social security number, credit cards, and other debts, such as mortgages, vehicle loans, and student loans. When a borrower cannot pay back a loan, the financial institution can report to any of the credit bureaus after a specified number of days. Then, the bureaus can record such defaults in the consumer's credit history, thus decreasing the borrower's creditworthiness and lowering the borrower's credit score. The reasoning is simple—the higher the credit score, the less risky you are in the eyes of the financial institutions. Good creditworthiness demonstrates to lenders that you are a financially responsible borrower. Conversely, the lower the credit score, the riskier you are to lenders, making it more difficult to qualify for loans. If the bases were loaded in the 9th inning, would you trust a hitter batting a **.100** average?

Naw, Bro Probably couldn't hit a tee ball...

The FICO Credit Scoring System

In 1989, the Fair Isaac Corporation, now known as FICO, introduced the credit score model widely used by most financial institutions today. The FICO scoring system is still popular, though each credit bureau may present differing FICO scores as they collect and report consumer credit information independently.

Excellent Versus Poor Creditworthiness

To understand the difference between an excellent credit score and a poor credit score, let's look at the FICO credit score ratings. A credit score can range from 300 to 850:

- 800-850 is Excellent
- 740-799 is Very Good
- 670-739 is Good
- 580-669 is Fair
- 300-579 as Poor

Wow, didn't know credit scores went that low...

Factors Determining Credit Scores

Learning the 5 factors of FICO's credit scoring model is crucial because they are the fundamental pillars of credit rating.

- 35% payment history
- 30% debt balance owed (credit utilization)
- 15% length of credit history

- 10% credit mix (credit diversity)
- 10% new accounts or recent credit inquiries

For the most part, consumers have the control over how their credit is shaped as long as they play by the rules of the credit rating system.

Payment History: 35%
The most critical factor, making up 35% of your credit score, is on-time debts payments. Undoubtedly, paying your bills on-time and not missing payment due dates can help build a healthy credit score. It's important to know that one missed payment can affect your credit score significantly. Payment history considers all the payments you've made or missed over time. Missing a payment is like missing practice, just imagine what coach would say!

Owe Naw... Coach would lose it!

The Credit Utilization Rule

"Consumers should use no more than 30% of their total available credit limit to maintain a healthy credit score."

Credit utilization is the amount of revolving consumer credit debt owed or used in relation to the total amount of consumer credit available and using over 30% can negatively impact your credit score. It's essential to understand *credit utilization* because it accounts for 30% of the FICO credit score. Let's go over some key terms to better understand credit utilization.

MVP Terms:
- Credit availability is the combined total of all revolving credit accounts, such as credit cards and lines of credit.

CHAPTER EIGHT

- Credit limit is the maximum amount of money lenders will allow borrowers to spend on a revolving credit account, such as a credit card or line of credit (LOC). *Adding the total limits of all credit lines, shows the total credit availability.

- Credit-debt balance is the amount used or spent on a revolving credit account, such as a credit card or line of credit.

Now, look at the table below to better understand credit utilization.

Credit Utilization Table Example:

Credit Cards	Credit Limit	Credit-Debt Balance
Amex	$25,000	$3,000
Discover	$10,000	$1,000
Chase	$15,000	$4,000
Apple Card	$12,000	$2,000
Totals	**$62,000**	**$10,000**

Total Credit Availability: $62,000
Total Credit-Debt Balance: $10,000

The credit utilization table shows a total available credit of $62,000 and a total debt balance of $10,000.

Find The Credit Utilization Ratio:

Calculate the credit utilization by dividing the total debt balance by the total available credit. Then multiply the result by 100 to find the percentage.

Divide: $10,000 credit-debt balance ÷ $62,000 total credit limit
Multiply: = 0.16 x 100
Score: = 16% credit utilization

WE GOOD!!

Credit utilization "weighs-in" nearly a third of a consumer's credit score in the FICO credit scoring system. A general rule for credit utilization is, the lower the ratio, the better! Below 30% is considered a healthy credit utilization ratio, and keeping a lower credit utilization further increases *credit availability,* decreases *credit debt balance* and interest paid. Ironically, lenders like to loan money to borrowers who DON'T need it.

Length Of Credit History: 15%
Credit history, which accounts for 15% of your credit score, refers to the length in which you've held credit accounts. When lenders are evaluating credit history, they are looking at the duration in which you've occupied installment loans and revolving credit debt. Therefore, the longer you've been in the credit game, the better, especially if you pay your debt obligations on time. In addition, your credit score will eventually improve with time as you build more credit history.

I'M ON THAT TYPE OF TIME!

Credit Diversification: 10%
Diversification of your credit accounts can help boost your credit score. It includes a mixture of different debts you have, such as credit cards, mortgages, vehicle loans, and student loans, etc. You want to be sure that your various credit accounts are being managed well and paid on time, or it will negatively affect your credit score.

New Accounts or Recent Credit Inquires: 10%
Taking on a new loan for the first time can affect your credit score in two ways. First, applying for new consumer credit cards and getting APPROVED, can increase your credit score because a new credit account increases the overall credit availability, thus lowering the credit utilization.

Conversely, when you have too many credit inquiries and new accounts within a short timeframe, it can raise questions about your financial situation. New accounts reveal to potential lenders that you are struggling financially and need high interest debt in order to maintain. Also, over applying for new accounts can drop your score by at least 2 to 4 points, even if approved. So it is best to be cautious when inquiring or applying for new credit accounts.

(Story Time...)

NBA legend, 5x Lakers Champion, and prolific business man, Earvin "Magic" Johnson, had the vision of entrepreneurship post his professional NBA career. Magic, who owned a chain of movie theaters, wanted to enter the food and beverage industry and had his sights on Starbucks, who was becoming a powerhouse. He saw the potential of the future Fortune 500 company and the lack of its representation in urban America. However, the process of securing enough capital to invest in Starbucks would be a lengthy because of the lack of credit—as he was asking for a $150 million loan in the mid 90s. After 3 years, eight banks declined Magic, except for a bank in Sacramento that gave him a $50 million loan to test his business acumen. Magic flipped the $50 million loan by refurbishing a strip mall, netting him a profit of $26 million. Seeing this, the bank granted Magic the remaining $100 million. He then joined forces with Howard Schultz, the CEO of Starbucks, to expand 125 stores across urban America. Learning that building credit is all about establishing relationships, Magic repaid the loan using just 20 of the 125 stores and later sold his stake in Starbucks for a $100 million gain. He now owns multi-billion dollar enterprise spanning 4 major sports franchises: MLB's Dodgers, NFL's Commanders, WNBA's LA Sparks, and MLS's LA Football Club.

HALF-TIME

Practice... Communicate... Believe

"A life is not important except in the impact it has on other lives."
— Jackie Robinson

The Vantage Credit Scoring System

The Vantage Scoring system was introduced in 2006 and was jointly developed by the three major credit bureaus. It was created as an alternative credit scoring model to FICO. Despite having less market share than FICO, the Vantage Score is becoming increasingly popular. The Vantage Score credit factors are:

- 40% payment history
- 34% amount owed (credit utilization)
- 21% depth of debt balances
- 5% new or recent credit inquires

Banks Have Their Own Internal Credit Reporting System??

Internal Ratings-Based Approach IRB

The internal ratings-based approach to credit risk allows banks to model their own conditions for calculating risk. The IRB allows banks to protect themselves from lending money to untrustworthy borrowers, regardless of their credit scores. It's always good practice, when borrowing from lenders, to ask about their internal credit rating system.

Business Credit Score

Dun & Bradstreet (D&B) is known as the leader in business credit reporting, much like the three consumer credit reporting bureaus. They achieved this by requiring businesses to obtain a D-U-N-S number by creating a business credit profile on their website.

A D-U-N-S number is a nine-digit identifier that is much like a social security number for businesses. Setting up a D&B credit profile gives companies a better understanding about your business, credit history, and creditworthiness. The purpose of a D-U-N-S number is to be an easy way for lending partners to evaluate a businesses creditworthiness when applying for loans, new contracts, and financing equipment. To obtain a D-U-N-S number, you will need the following:

- a legal name
- headquarters name and address for your business
- Doing Business As (DBA) or other names the business is recognized by
- physical address
- mailing address (If separate from headquarters and/or physical address)
- telephone number
- contact name and title
- number of employees at the business's physical location
- whether it's a home-based business

What Can Lower A Credit Score

Understanding the reasons that can lower your credit score is just as important as knowing what can improve it. Let's start with the negatives because it is essential to avoid behaviors that lead to poor credit.

Missing Payments

DEFENSE TO OFFENSE, I LIKE IT...

One of the leading factors causing credit scores to plummet is missing payments. As previously mentioned, 35% of what affects your credit score is payment history. This shows how important lenders and banks view on-time payments. When you miss a payment, there is usually a grace period of 30 days; however, lenders allow this as a courtesy. If the lender does not receive payment by the due date per the loan agreement, then the debt is considered delinquent and may be subject to negative credit reporting.

High Credit Utilization

Even though using credit is a useful strategy to build credit, avoid maxing out your credit accounts. Credit bureaus consider high credit utilization as a red flag. Too many credit lines with high utilization, gives the impression that you are constantly looking to borrow money. Lenders want borrowers who do not NEED money, so be sure not to exceed a 30% credit utilization ratio.

Almost Ran it Up!

Defaulting

When you default on credit accounts, this can be an enormous problem down the road, especially for your credit score. Defaulting includes bankruptcies, repossessions, charge-offs, collections, and foreclosures. Defaulting can lower your credit score by hundreds of points and can have a negative impact on your credit score for many years.

Too Many Credit Inquiries: Hard vs Soft Inquires

The credit bureaus record *"hard inquiries"* when you apply for a new credit accounts. Too many hard inquiries shows lenders you are financially unstable and too dependent on credit. This is because individuals with 6 or more recent hard inquires are 8 times more likely to file bankruptcy. You should try to limit your credit inquires to 1 to 3 a year. Also, every inquire lowers your credit score by 2 to 4 points. *"Soft inquiries"* conducted during a pre-approval will not affect the credit score but will take time to fall off.

Hey, You Got To Shoot Your Shot...

How To Improve Your Credit Score

Now let's look through some ways to improve and build a healthy credit score. By taking action to increase your credit score and showing creditworthiness to lenders, this will save you a significant amount of money over time.

Profile Identity

With over 340 million people in the U.S. and 8 billion people on the planet, this increases the likelihood of sharing the same name and the possibility that the wrong debt can appear on your credit profile. Start by calling each credit bureau to double check that your first, middle, and last name, as well as your home address, is accurate to mitigate credit reported discrepancies. The accuracy of your profile identity is one of the most overlooked ways to improve your credit score.

On-Time Payments

If missing a payment is one of the largest factors to lower credit, then timely payments have to be one of the largest factors to improve credit. Be sure to make your debt and expense payments on time to avoid delinquencies. Also, double down by automating bill payments or scheduling reminders a week before the payment due date. Automatic payments reduces the likelihood of missing payment obligations.

Avoid Closing Credit Accounts

Like opening new credit accounts, closing existing credit accounts could negatively affect your credit score as well. That's because, by closing a credit account, it lowers the credit availability, increases the credit utilization, and no longer counts towards your credit history. If you are not using a particular credit card, it is best to keep the credit card open and in a safe place. You will need to monitor the credit card every six months to ensure no fraudulent activity has occurred.

Credit Diversification or Credit Mix
Credit diversification refers to the different credit accounts on a consumer's credit profile. Maintaining multiple accounts such as mortgages, vehicle loans, and credit cards over a period of time shows lenders that you are responsible borrower with the ability to manage a variety of debt.

Tradeline

A credit tradeline is a single account listing on an individual's credit profile. When you open a new credit card, purchase a vehicle, or finance equipment for a business, you are opening a new *tradeline,*— or *credit account.* Tradelines contain detailed information about your account, such as payment history, utilization, and the type of tradeline it is. There are three types of trade lines. First is the most common, *revolving credit*—which includes credit cards and lines of credit (LOC). Second is *installment loans* such as personal loans, mortgages, vehicle loans, and student loans. Third is *open accounts* for financed items like work equipment and furniture.

Joint Accounts
Whenever two individuals co-sign for a tradeline like a vehicle purchase, the tradeline appears on both party's credit report. Sometimes a co-signer, or joint applicant, is required for individuals who otherwise would not have qualified for the loan on their own. Adding a co-signer usually happens at the point of sale or closing date, and is more common with installment loans and open accounts.

Co-signers for revolving credit accounts such as credit cards and lines of credit (LOC), are typically not needed. Lenders make it easy for single borrowers to get approved and add additional users to the account if necessary. That's because banks and credit card companies will reduce the funds available to approved borrowers with less than desirable credit. Once the credit account is established, borrowers can choose to add co-signers or authorized users to their revolving credit account.

Why Is This Important?
It's important to note that a co-signer, or joint applicant, is not the same as an authorized user on the account. Typically, an authorized user on a credit account is a family member, partner, or child over 15 who has been given access to a tradeline for emergency funds. An authorized user may assume a portion or all the credit history of the original card owner. This could potentially boost or reduce the authorized user's credit score.

However, authorized users do not share the same liability as the original card owner or co-signing joint applicant. Authorized users can make purchases to the credit account without being held liable for repayment. All the liability for debt repayment is on the original owner or co-signer of the account. So, it's important to be sure that the joint applicants or authorized users are trustworthy before adding them to your credit profile to remain financially efficient.

I MADE IT!!!

"Anything is possible. ANYTHING IS POSSIBLE!"
— Kevin Garnett

I Knew You Could Do It!

FINAL CHAPTER:
→

9

The Most Important Analytic

Health.

"The health is the most important thing and we have to take care of our bodies, our mind—in a spiritual way as well. It doesn't matter about cultures or religions because we are all the same... It doesn't matter the age, it's about what you give to your mind and your body."
— Cristiano Ronaldo

Made in the USA
Columbia, SC
17 February 2025